GREAT MEDIEVAL CHURCHES AND CATHEDRALS OF EUROPE

120 Classic Engravings

Jules Gailhabaud

DOVER PUBLICATIONS, INC.
Mineola, New York

Bibliographical Note

This Dover edition, first published in 2002, is an original selection of plates republished from *Monuments Ancients et Modernes,* originally published by Librairie de Firmin Didot Frères, Paris, 1853.

DOVER *Pictorial Archive* SERIES

Library of Congress Cataloging-in-Publication Data

Gailhabaud, Jules, 1810–1888.
    [Monuments ancients et modernes. English. Selections]
    Great medieval churches and cathedrals of Europe: 120 classic engravings / Jules Gailhabaud.
        p. cm. — (Dover pictorial archive series)
    "Selection of plates republished from Monuments ancients et modernes, originally published by Librairie de Firmin Didot Frères, 1853"—T.p. verso.
    ISBN 0-486-42333-6 (pbk.)
     1. Church architecture—Pictorial works. 2. Architecture, Medieval—Pictorial works. 3. Engraving, French—19th century. I. Title. II. Series.
NA5453 .G3513 2002
726.5'09'02022—dc21
                                           2002067322

Manufactured in the United States of America
Dover Publications, Inc., 31 East 2nd Street, Mineola, N.Y. 11501

Publisher's Note

From the humblest village chapel to the soaring majesty of the great Gothic cathedrals, the ecclesiastical buildings of Europe in the Middle Ages were visible symbols of the power and authority of the church as well as places of refuge, sanctity and salvation for parishioners across the social spectrum—from serf to seigneur. The design and construction of churches–cathedrals in particular–employed a vast range of workers—architects, masons, carpenters, sculptors, glass workers, woodcarvers and unskilled laborers, who toiled for years—often for a lifetime—to erect these edifices dedicated to the glory of God.

This collection of 120 masterly engravings offers a rich pictorial overview of the ecclesiastical architecture of the Middle Ages. The plates have been reproduced from a monumental four-volume study published in 1853 by French archaeologist Jules Gailhabaud and dedicated to Louis-Napoléon Bonaparte. While the complete work encompasses architecture from all eras and locales, the plates reproduced here deal exclusively with medieval churches and cathedrals. Almost all are located in Europe.

Spanning over a thousand years of history, these classic engravings offer revealing insights into the evolution and diversity of religious architecture in the Christian West, from the Latin basilica forms of such early structures as the Basilica of St. Saba in Rome, and the Church of Grotta Ferrata, through the Romanesque glories of Strasbourg Cathedral and the Byzantine splendor of the Church of St. Vitale at Ravenna, to the apotheosis of Gothic grandeur in the magnificent cathedrals of Notre Dame (Paris) and Amiens in France, Germany's Cologne Cathedral, and York Minster and Salisbury Cathedral in England.

Highly detailed, the plates comprise interior and exterior views, cross sections, elevations, floor plans, and more, providing not only a rich visual overview of medieval church architecture, but clear, accurate representations of altars, pulpits, thrones, tombs, fonts, cloisters, bays, stalls, choirs, windows, statuary, and many other features and elements of church design. Any student of ecclesiastical architecture, medieval life, church history, or devotional life in the Middle Ages will want to study this outstanding collection of plates. Artists and illustrators will also appreciate the fine detail and authenticity of these splendid engravings, which may be reproduced without permission or fee.

List of Churches and Cathedrals by Country

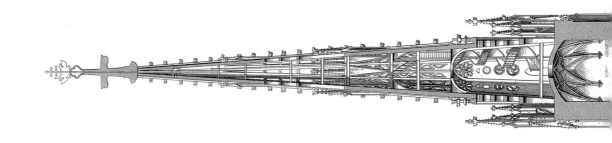
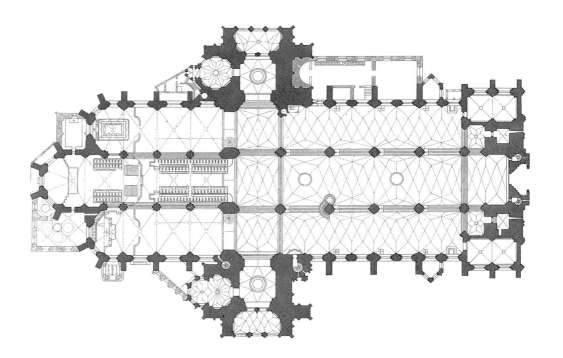

Echelle pour le Plan.

Echelle pour la Coupe.

Plate 1

Church of St. Stephen, Vienna, Austria
Plan and Cross Section

Plate 2

Church of St. Stephen
Longitudinal Section

20 Mètres

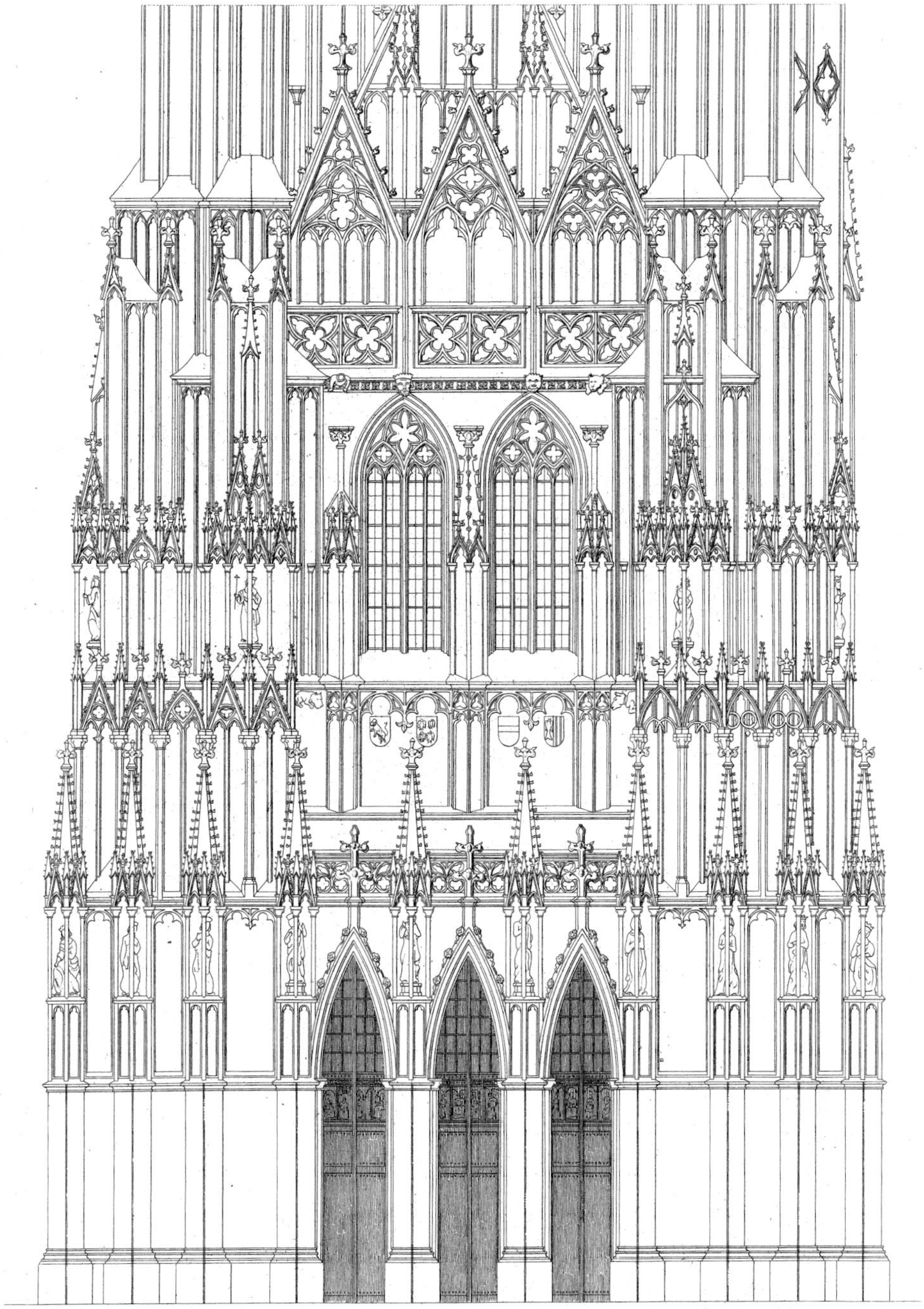

Fig. 1.

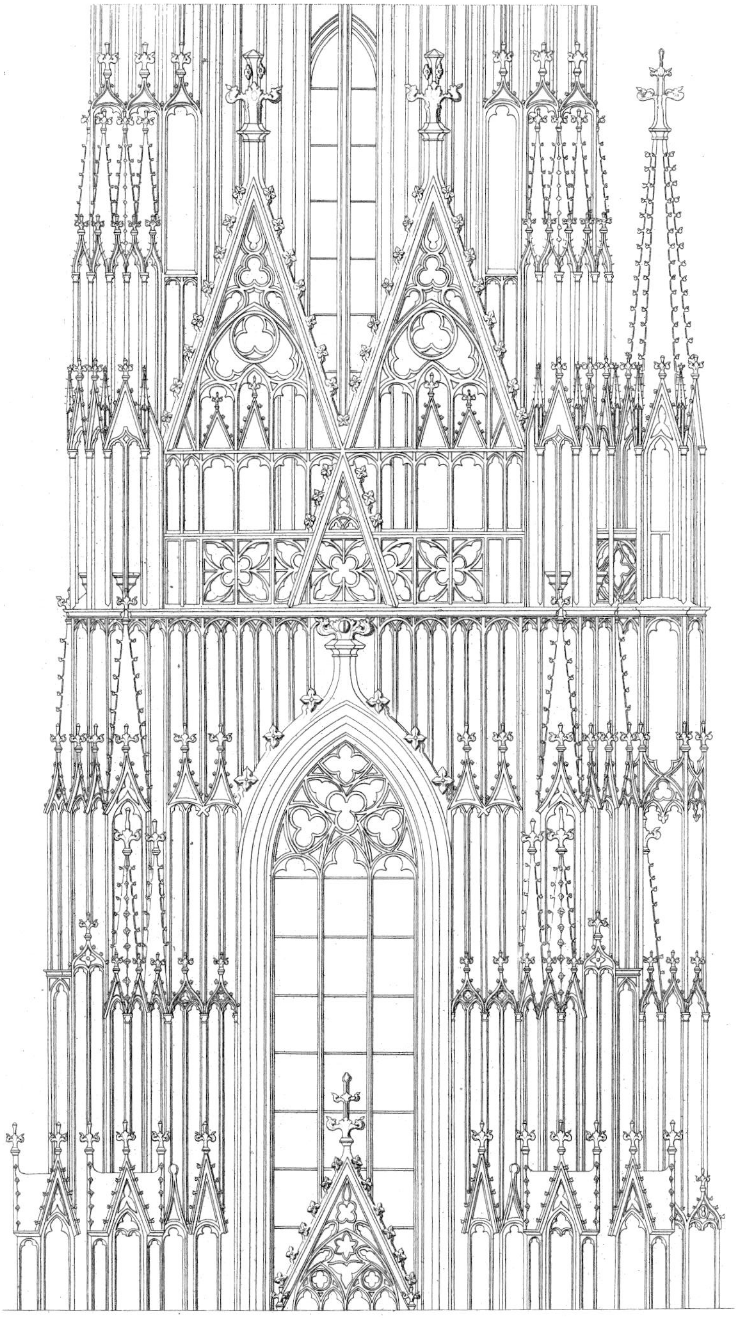

Fig. 2.

Plate 3

Church of St. Stephen
Details

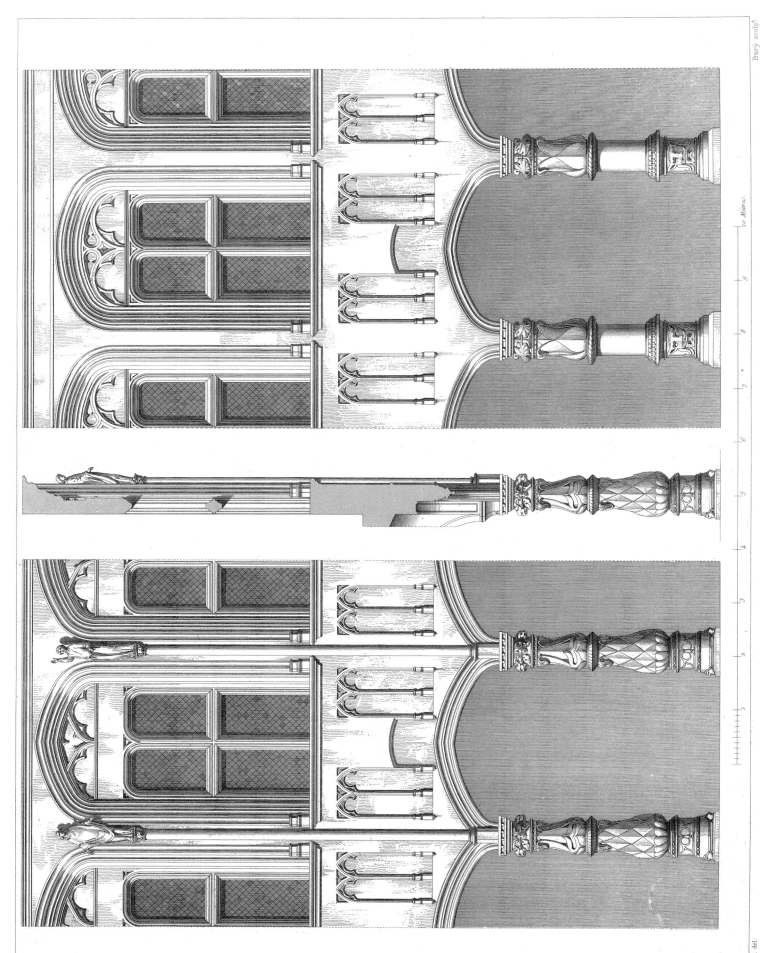

Anoudru del.   Bury sculp.ᵗ

Plate 4

Episcopal Palace, Liège, Belgium
Elevations of the Piers

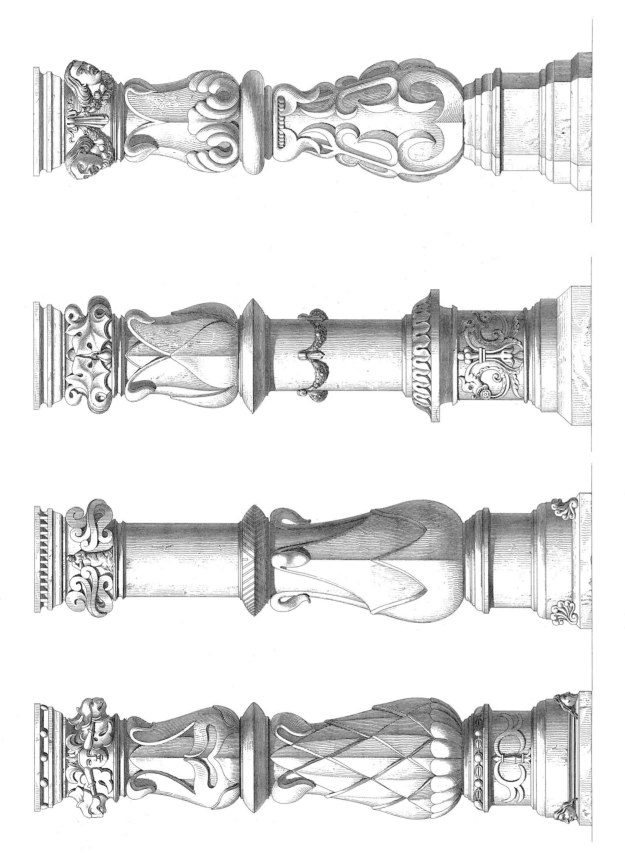

Plate 5

Episcopal Palace, Liège
Details

A. Berty del.

Bury sculp.[t]

Plate 6

St. Botolph's Church, Boston, England

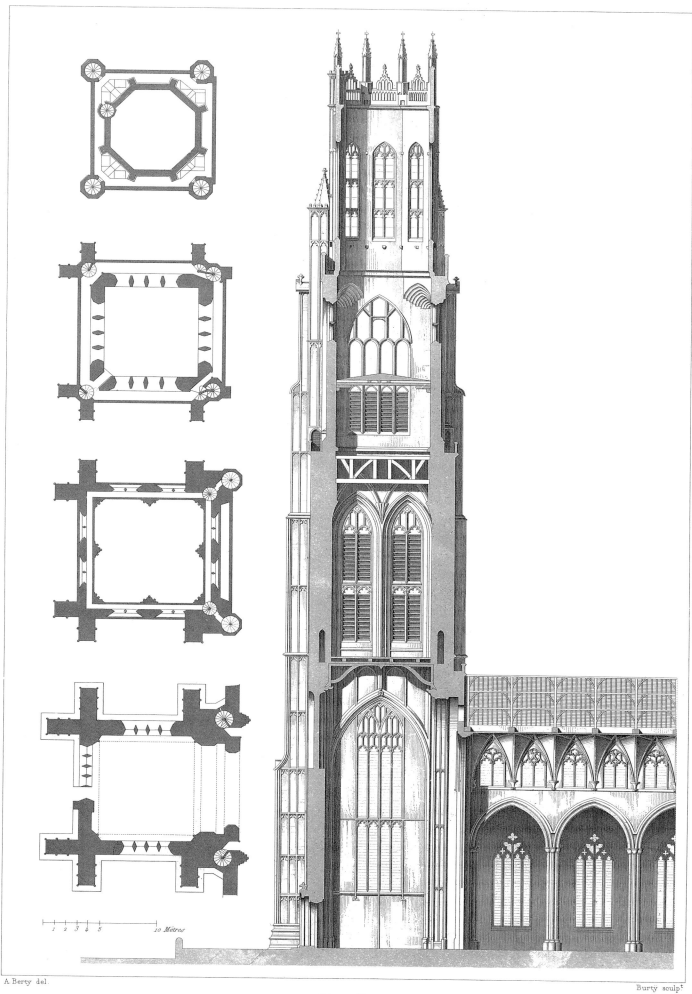

A. Berty del.

Burty sculp.

Plate 7

St. Botolph's Church
Details

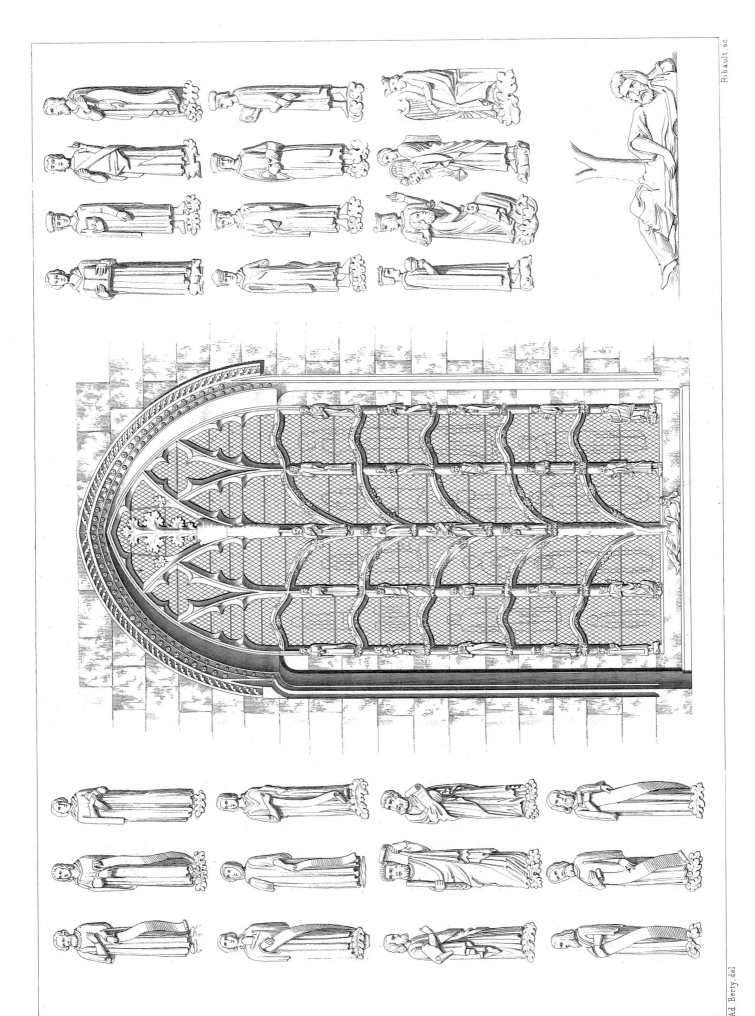

Ad Berty. del

Ribault. sc

Plate 8

Dorchester Church, Oxfordshire, England

Ad. Berty del.

Bury sculp.

Plate 9

Hadiscoe Church, England

Echelle p.^r la Fig 1

4   8 Mètres

Echelle p.^r la Fig. 3

4   8 Mètres

Fig. 1.

Fig. 2.

Fig. 3.

Berty del.

Bury sculp.^t

Plate 10

Crypts at Lastingham, Oxford (England), and Issoire (France)

A. Berty del.

Bury sculp

Plate 11

Salisbury Cathedral, England
Chapter-Room

Plate 12

Tomb of Bishop Bridport, Salisbury, England

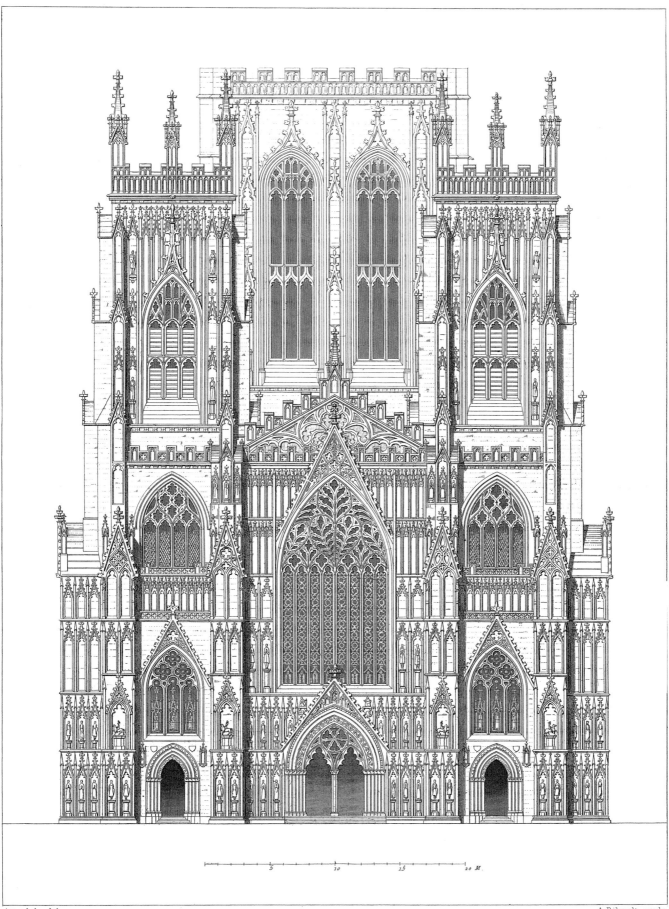

Plate 13

Cathedral, York, England
Elevation of the Facade

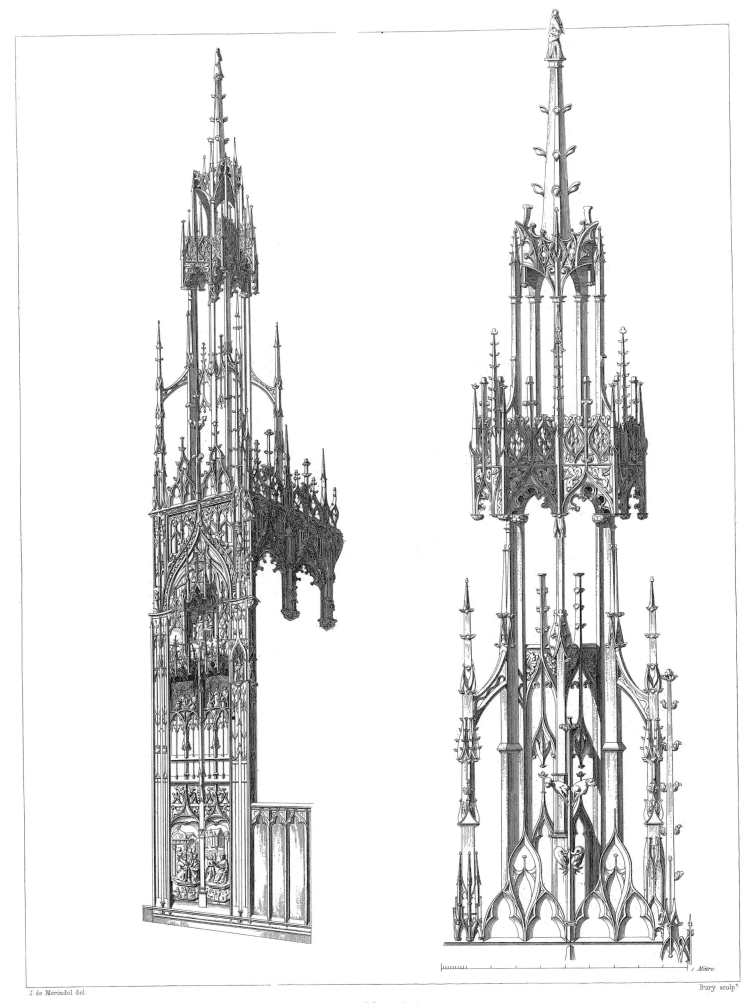

1 Mètre.

Plate 14

Cathedral, Amiens, France
Stalls

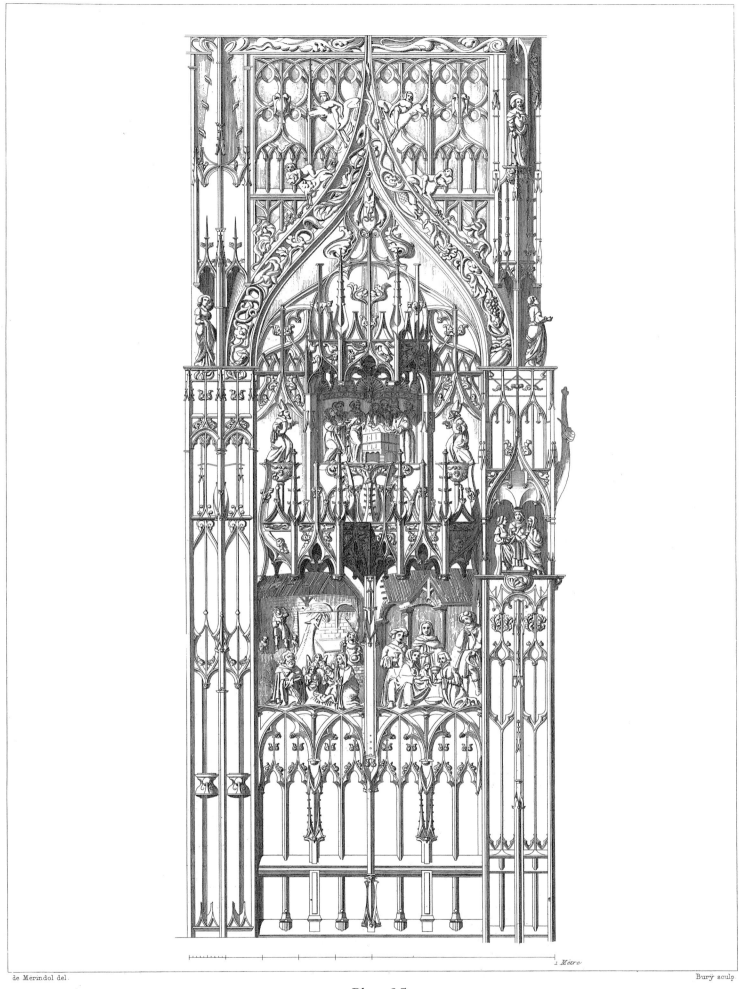

1 Mètre

Plate 15

Amiens Cathedral
Elevation, Stalls

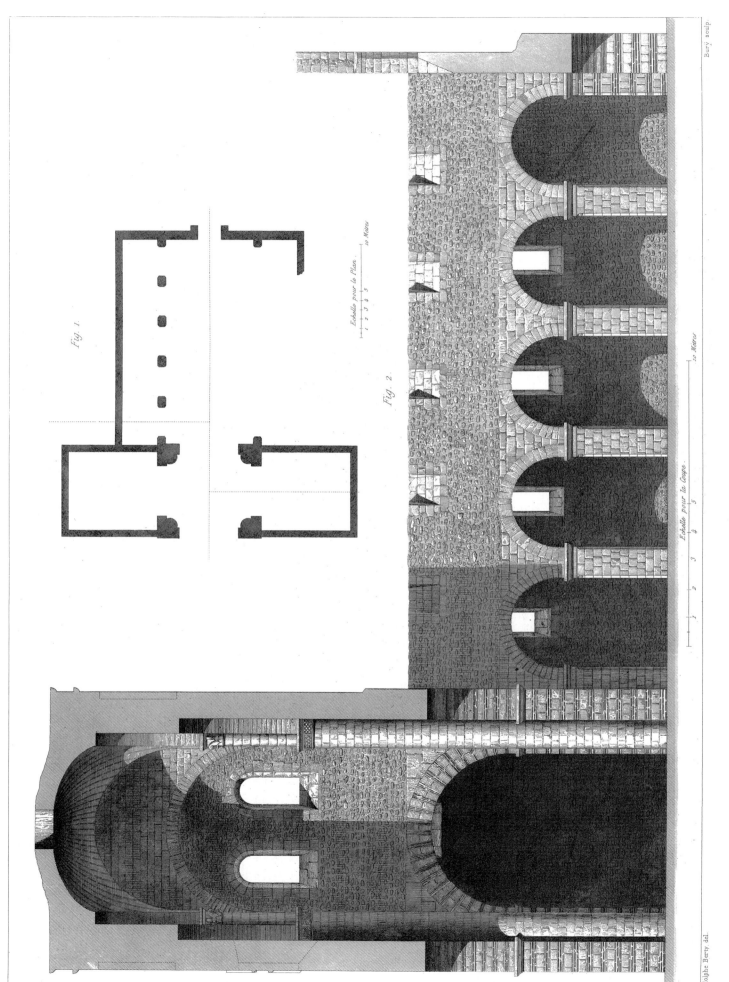

Fig. 1.

Fig. 2.

Echelle pour le Plan.

10 Metres

Echelle pour la Coupe.

10 Metres

Adolphe Berty del.

Bury sculp.

Plate 16

St. Martin's Church, Angers, France
Plan and Cross Section

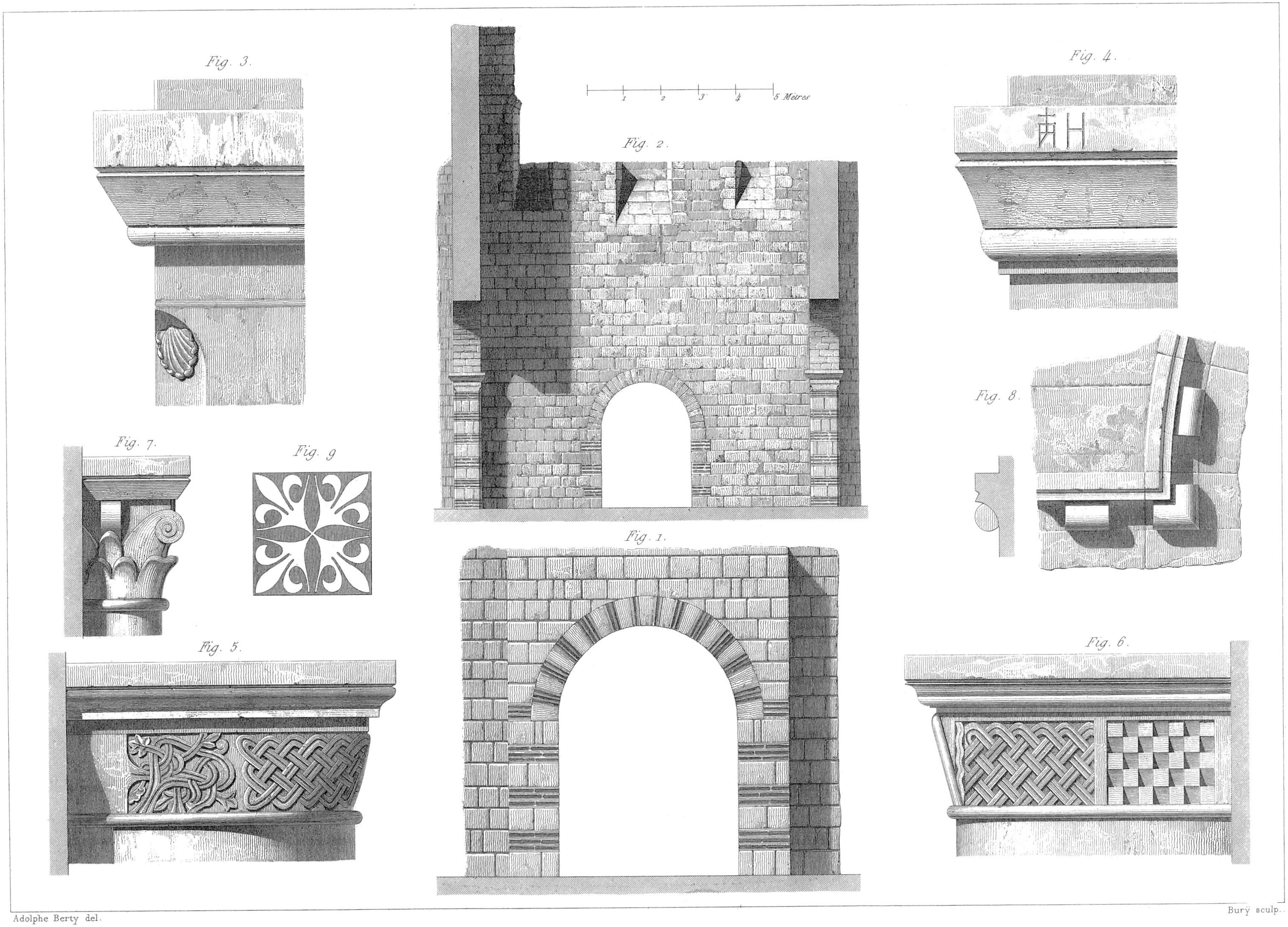
Fig. 3.
Fig. 4.
1 2 3 4 5 Mètres
Fig. 2.
Fig. 7.
Fig. 9
Fig. 8.
Fig. 1.
Fig. 5.
Fig. 6.
Adolphe Berty del.
Bury sculp.

Plate 17

St. Martin's Church, Angers
Details

Plate 18

Cathedral, Bourges, France
South Porch

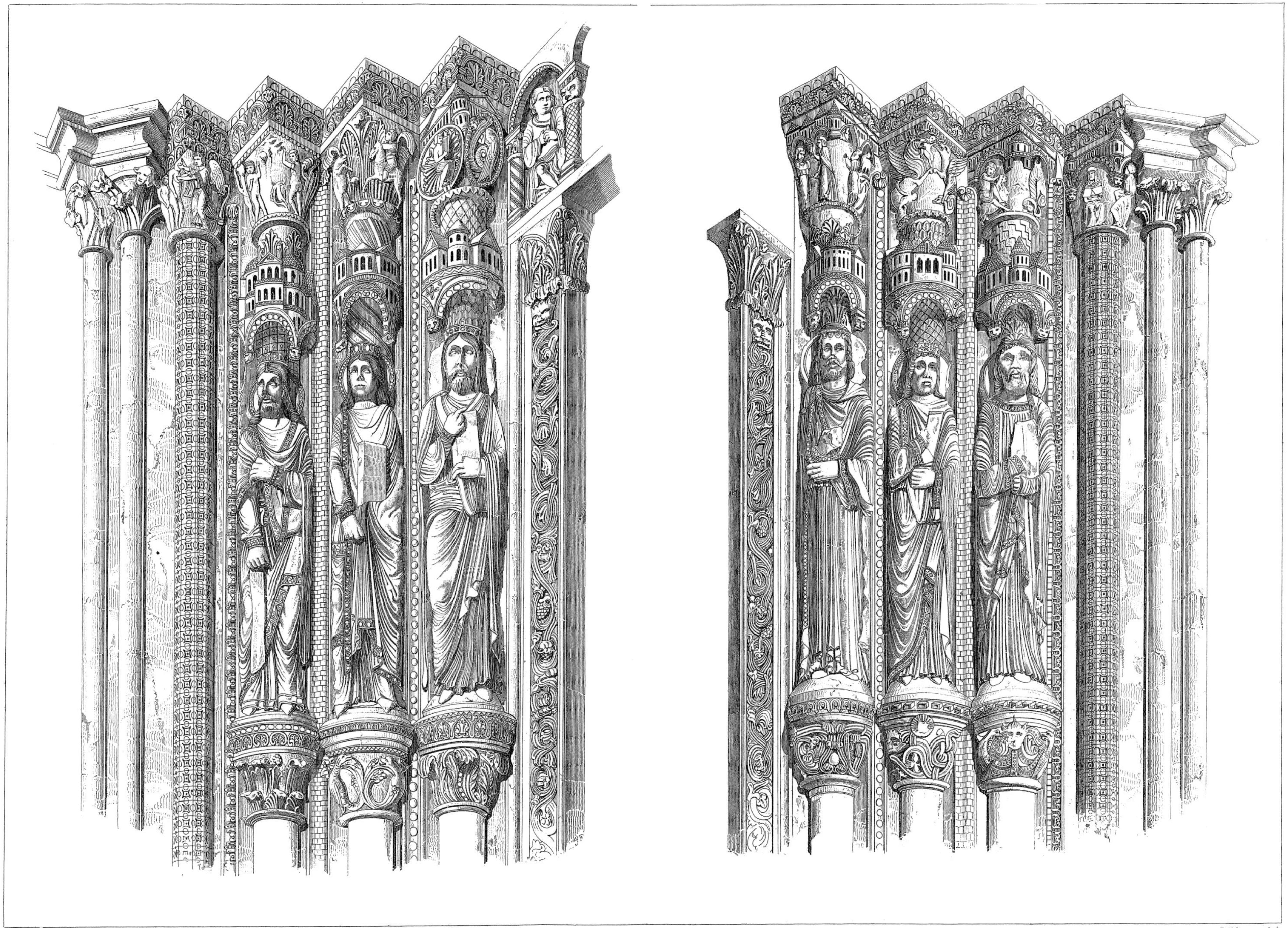

J. de Mérindol del

R. Pfnor sculpt.

Plate 19

Bourges Cathedral
Details, South Porch

20 Metres.

10

Plate 20

Church of Notre-Dame-du-Port, Clermont, France
Lateral Elevation

E. Viollet Leduc del.

Lemaitre sculp.t

Plate 21

Church of Notre-Dame-du-Port, Clermont
Longitudinal Section

K. Boesvilvald del.

1 0 1 2 3 4 5 10 Métres

Bury sculp.ᵗ

Plate 22

Church of Marmoutier, France

Fig. 3.

Fig. 7.

Fig. 4.

Fig. 8.

Fig. 5.

Fig. 9.

Fig. 6.

Fig. 10.

Fig. 2.

Fig. 1.

1 2 3 4 5 6 7 8 9 10 Mètres

E. Boesvilvald del.

Bury sculpt.

Plate 23

Church of Marmoutier
Details

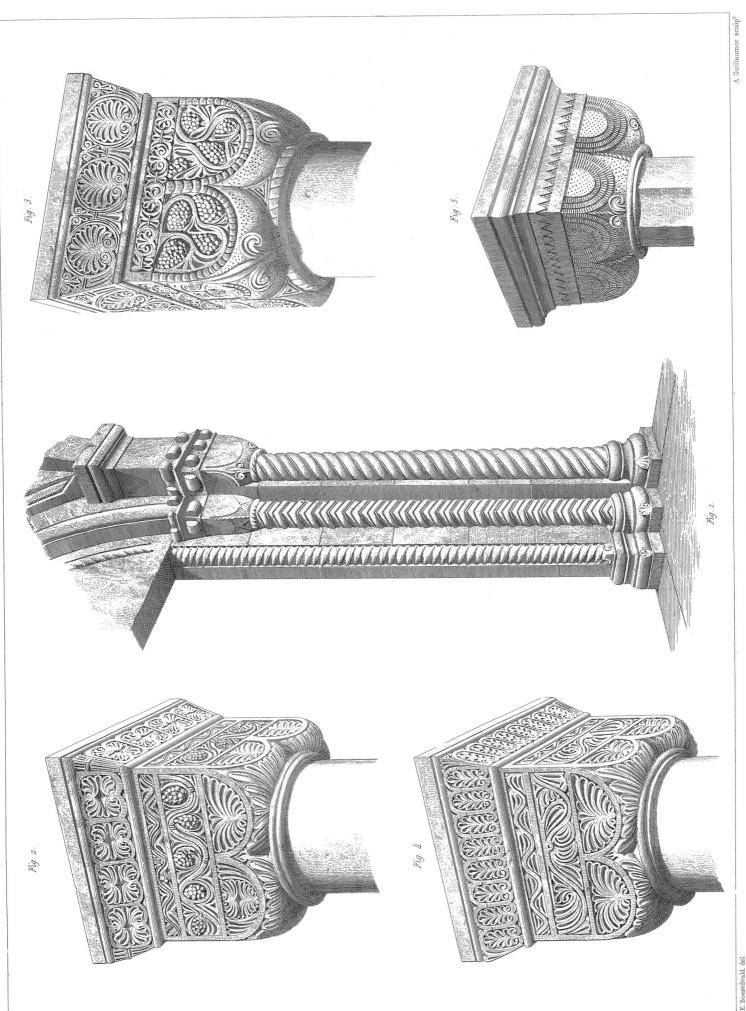

Fig. 3.

Fig. 5.

Fig. 1.

Fig. 2.

Fig. 4.

Plate 24

Church of Marmoutier
Details

Fig. 2.

Fig. 1.

Fig. 3.

Fig. 4.

Fig. 5.

Fig. 6.

Fig. 7.

Fig. 8.

Fig. 9.

Fig. 10.

Fig. 11.

Fig. 12.

Fig. 13.

Fig. 14.

Fig. 15.

Fig. 16.

Fig. 17.

Fig. 18.

Fig. 19.

Fig. 20.

Fig. 21.

Fig. 22.

Fig. 23.

E. Boesvilvald del.

A. Guillaumot sculp.

Plate 25

Church of Marmoutier
Details

MARTIRIO SCSPE

A. Berty del.

Bury sculp.

Plate 26

Cloisters of the Abbey, Moissac, France

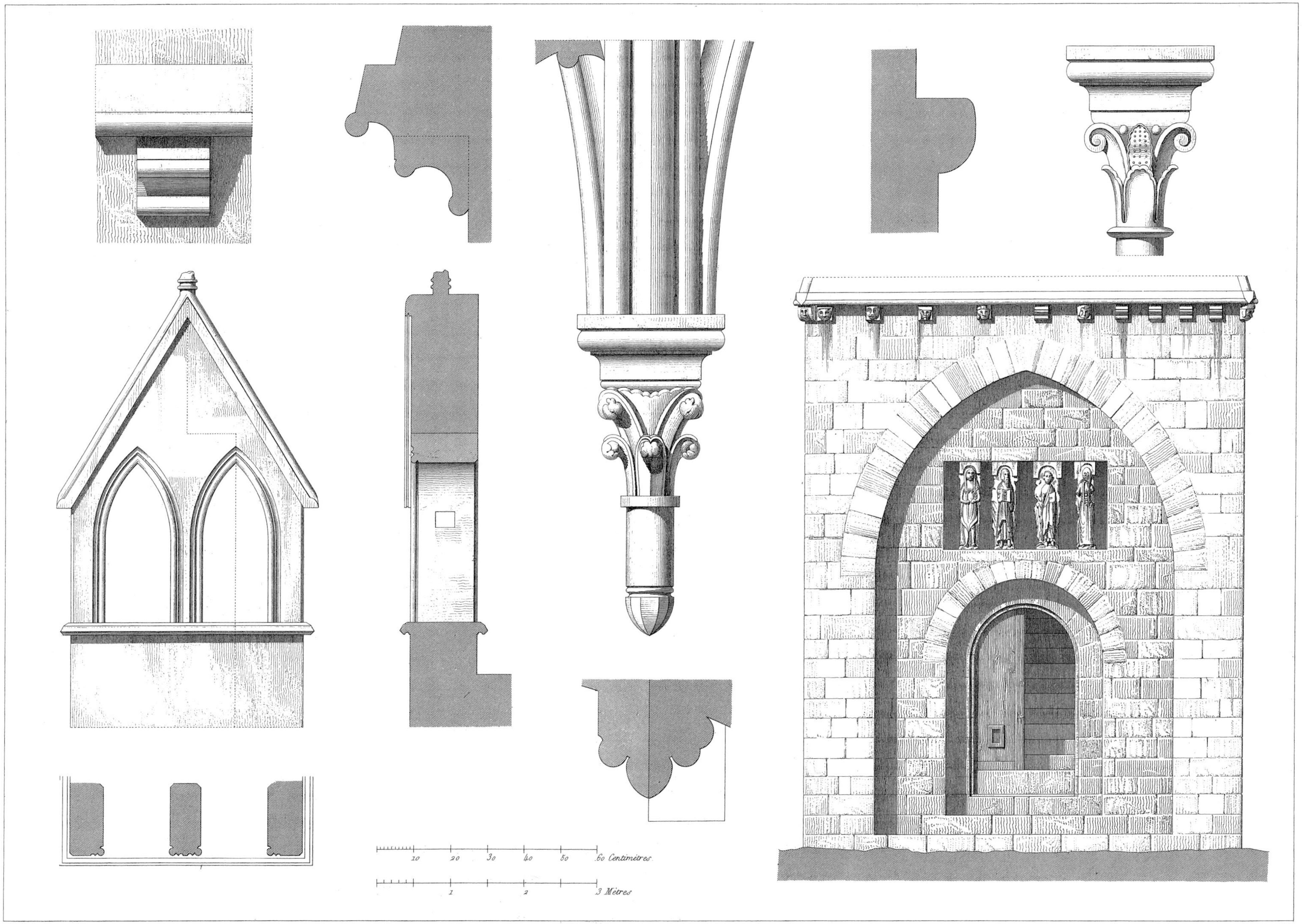

Adolphe Berty del

Bury sculp.t

Plate 27

Sepulchral Chapel, Montmorillon, France
Details

Ad Berty, del

Ribault, sc.

Plate 28

Cathedral of Notre Dame, Paris, France
Enclosure of the Choir

Plate 29

Cathedral of Notre Dame
Elevation of Bay, Enclosure of the Choir

Ad. Berty. del.

Ribault. sc.

Plate 30

Cathedral of Notre Dame
South Bay, Enclosure of the Choir

E. Viollet Leduc del.

Burÿ et Schrœder sculp.

Plate 31

Church of St. Front, Périguex, France

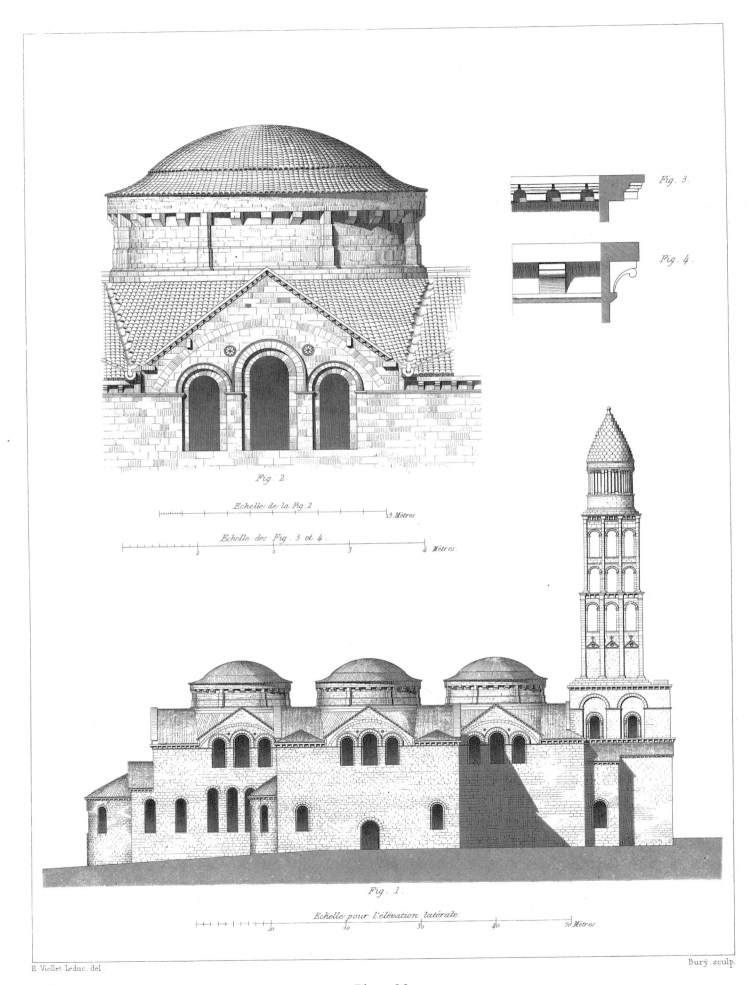

Fig. 3.

Fig. 4.

Fig. 2.

Echelle de la Fig. 2

33 Mètres

Echelle des Fig. 3 et 4.

1   2   3   4 Mètres.

Fig. 1.

Echelle pour l'élévation latérale

10   20   30   40   50 Mètres.

E. Viollet Leduc. del.

Bury. sculp.

Plate 32

Church of St. Front
Details

Fig. 1

Fig. 2

Fig. 3

Fig. 4

Fig. 5

Fig. 6

Fig. 7

Echelle pour la Fig. 5.

1 2 3 4 5 6 M.

Echelle pour les Fig. 2.3.4.

1 2 2 M.

Echelle pour la Fig. 1.

1 2 3 4 5 6 M.

E. Viollet Leduc del.

Bury sculps

Plate 33

Church of St. Front
Details

Plate 34

Baptistery, Poitiers, France
Elevation

Fig. 5.

Fig. 6 bis.

Fig. 6

Fig. 4.

Fig. 2 bis.

Fig. 2.

Fig. 7.

Fig. 3.

Fig. 1.

Fig. 8.

Ad. Berty del.

Burr sculp.

1 Metre

Plate 35

Baptistery, Poitiers
Details of Elevation

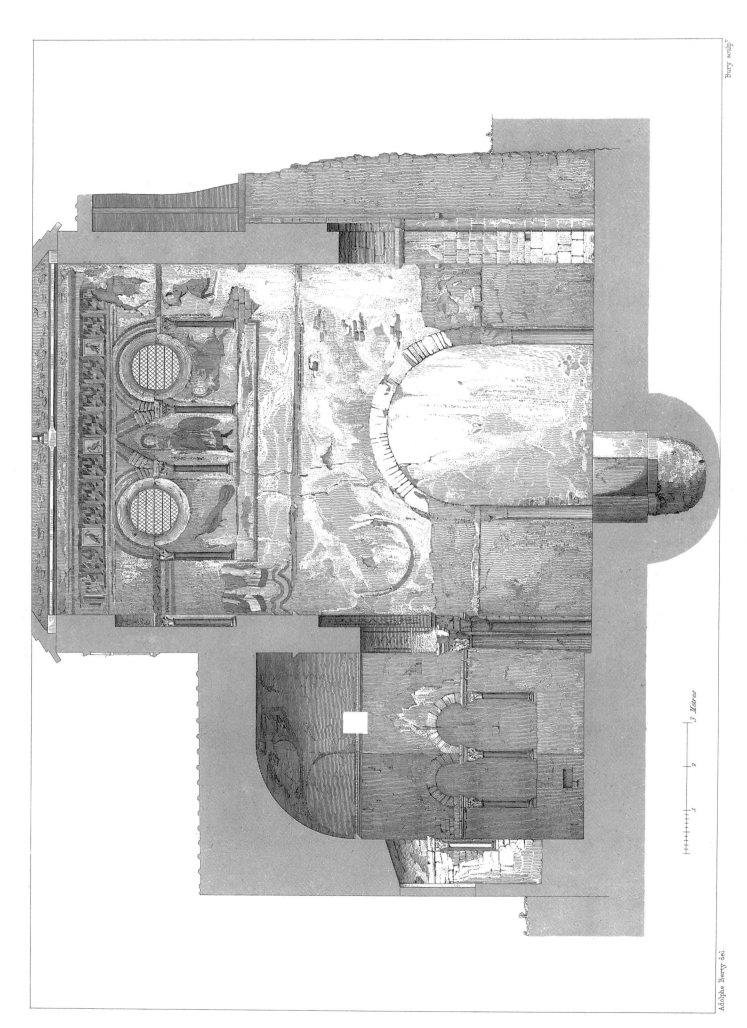

Plate 36

Baptistery, Poitiers
Longitudinal Section

3 Metres

Plate 37

Baptistery, Poitiers
Cross Section

D apres Mr Deroy

J Jourdan del.

Bury sculp^t

Plate 38

Church of Royat, France

Fig. 3.

Fig. 2.

Fig. 1.

Plate 39

Church of Savenières, France

J. Amoudru del.   Pfnor sculp.[t]

Plate 40

Organ of Strasbourg Cathedral

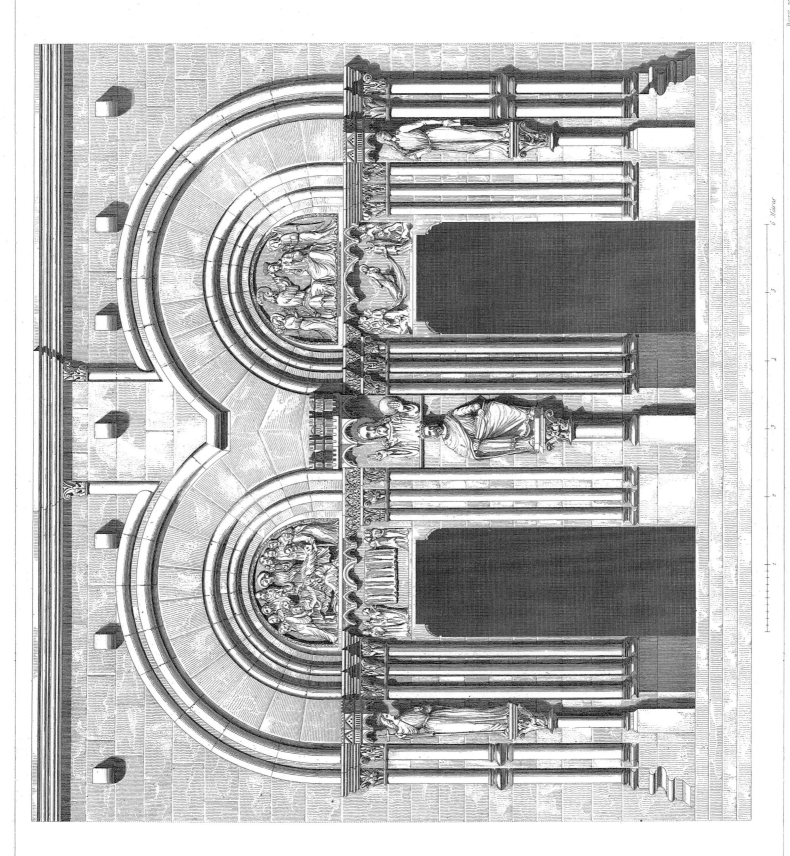

Plate 41

Cathedral, Strasbourg, France

J.Jourdan del.

d'après Ch. Fichot.

J.Bury sculp.

Plate 42

Magdalen Church, Troyes, France
Gallery

Plate 43

Cathedral, Bonn, Germany

Leveil del.

Bury sculp.^t

Plate 44

Cathedral, Cologne, Germany

Jourdan del.

Bury sculpt.

Plate 45

Cologne Cathedral
Elevation

Plate 46

Cologne Cathedral
Cross Section

Jourdan del.

J. Burÿ sc.

Plate 47

Cologne Cathedral
Longitudinal Section of Choir

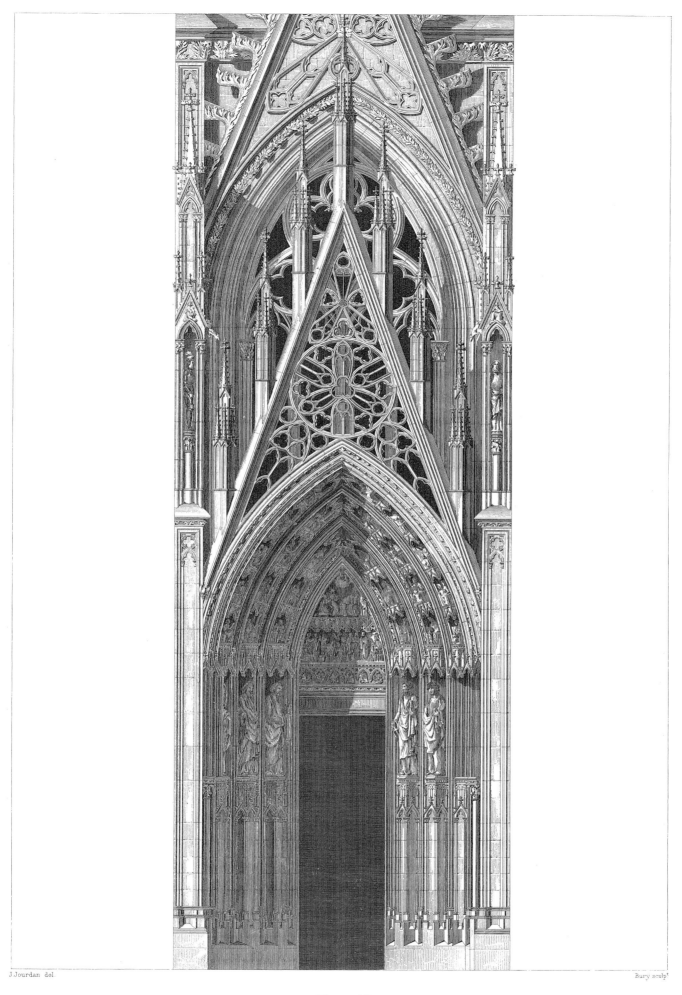

J.Jourdan del.

Bury sculp.

Plate 48

Cologne Cathedral
Details

Echelle pour la Fenêtre.

Jourdan del.

Bury sculpt.

Plate 49

Cologne Cathedral
Windows and Parts of Buttresses

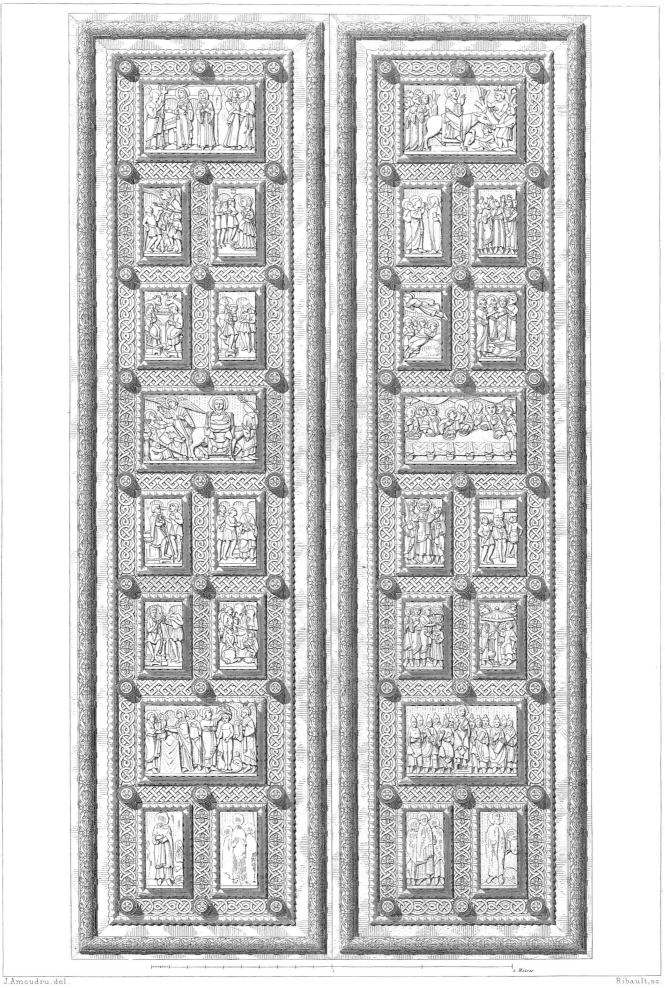

J.Amoudru.del.

Ribault,sc.

Plate 50

Church of St. Mary of the Capitol, Cologne, Germany
Door

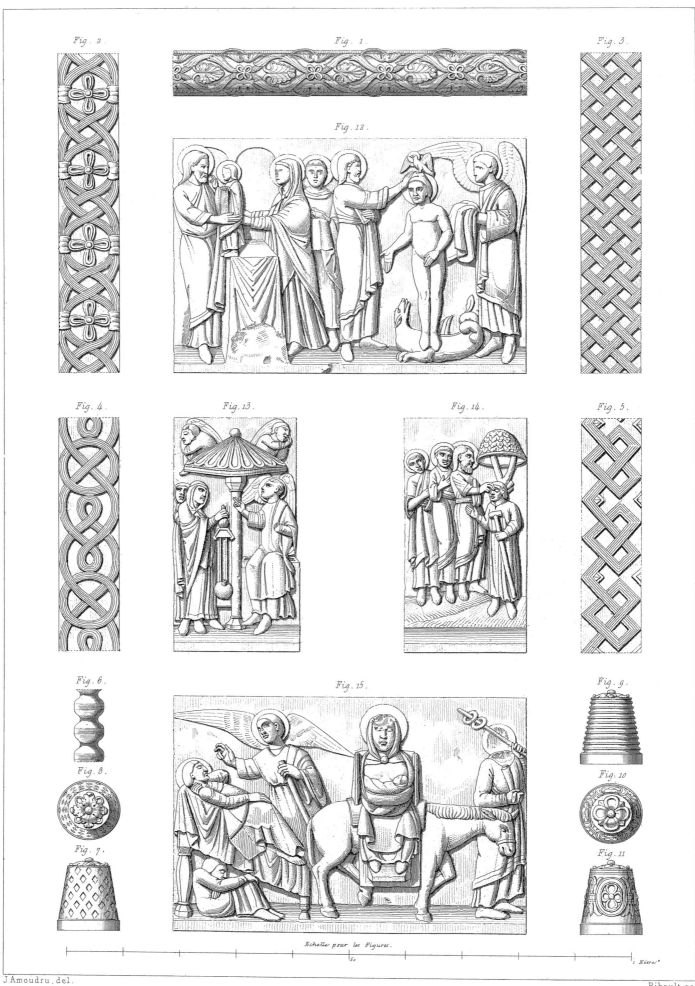

Fig. 2. Fig. 1. Fig. 3.

Fig. 12.

Fig. 4. Fig. 13. Fig. 14. Fig. 5.

Fig. 6. Fig. 15. Fig. 9.

Fig. 8. Fig. 10.

Fig. 7. Fig. 11.

Echelle pour les Figures.

J. Amoudru, del. Ribault, sc.

Plate 51

Church of St. Mary of the Capitol, Cologne
Details, Door

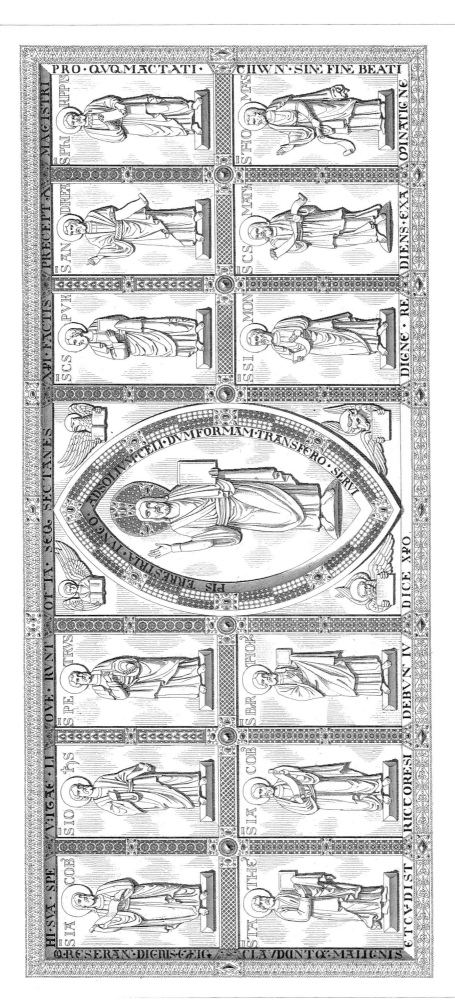

Plate 52

Church of Combourg, Germany
Altar-Piece

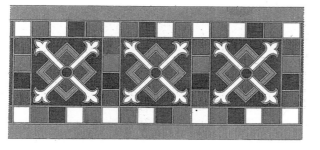

Plate 53

Church of Combourg
Enamel, Altar-piece

d'après Quaglio.

J. Burÿ del. et sculp.

Plate 54

Cathedral, Freiburg, Germany

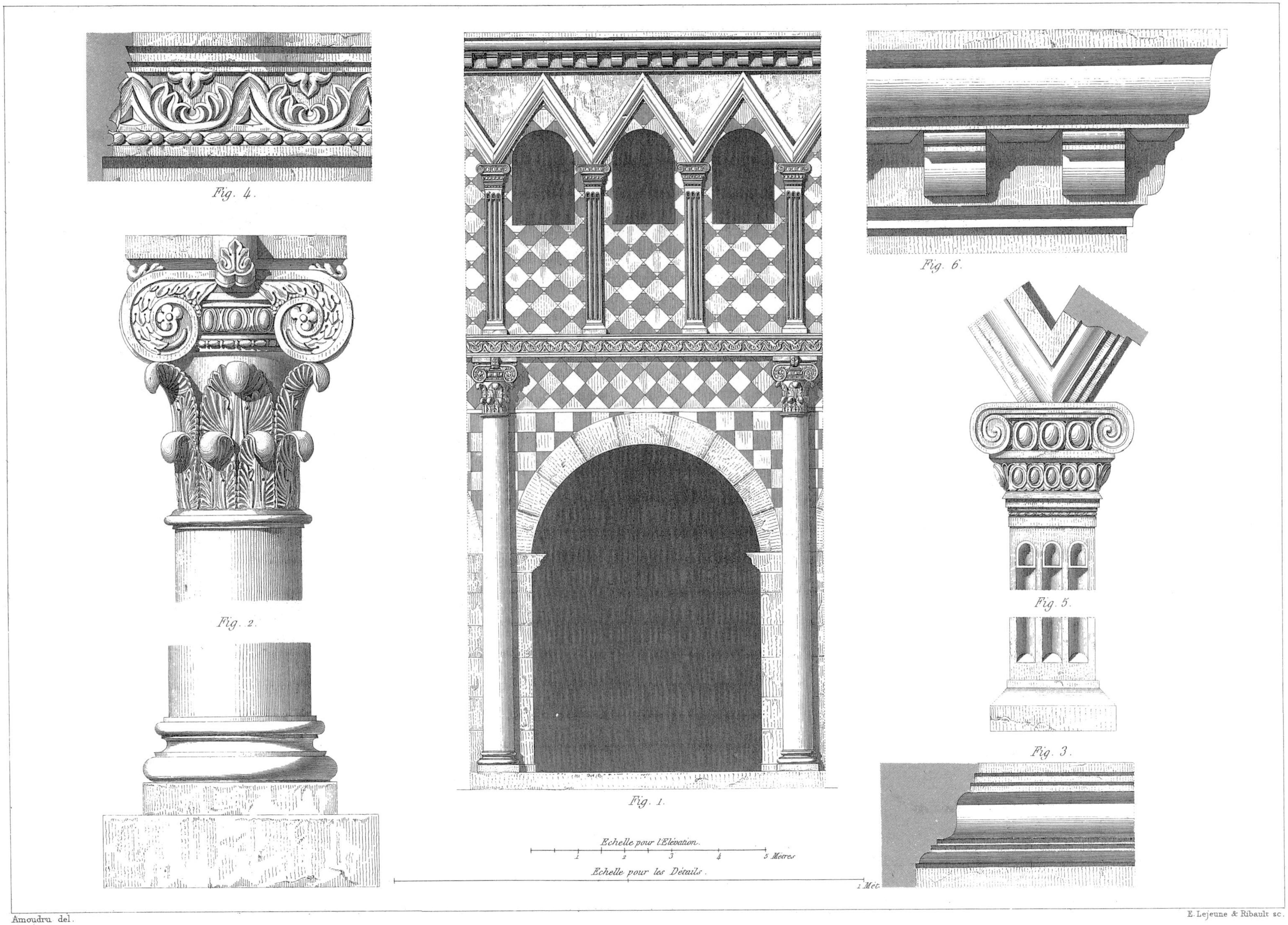
Fig. 4.
Fig. 2.
Fig. 1.
Fig. 6.
Fig. 5.
Fig. 3.
Echelle pour l'Elévation.
1
2
3
4
5 Mètres
Echelle pour les Détails.
1 Mèt.

Amoudru del.

E. Lejeune & Ribault sc.

Plate 55

Church of Lorsch, Germany
Porch of the Atrium

Plate 56

Cathedral, Mainz, Germany

Echelle du Plan.

10   20   40 M.

Echelle de l'Elevation.

5   10   20 M.

Amoudru del.

Plate 57

Mainz Cathedral, Germany
Details

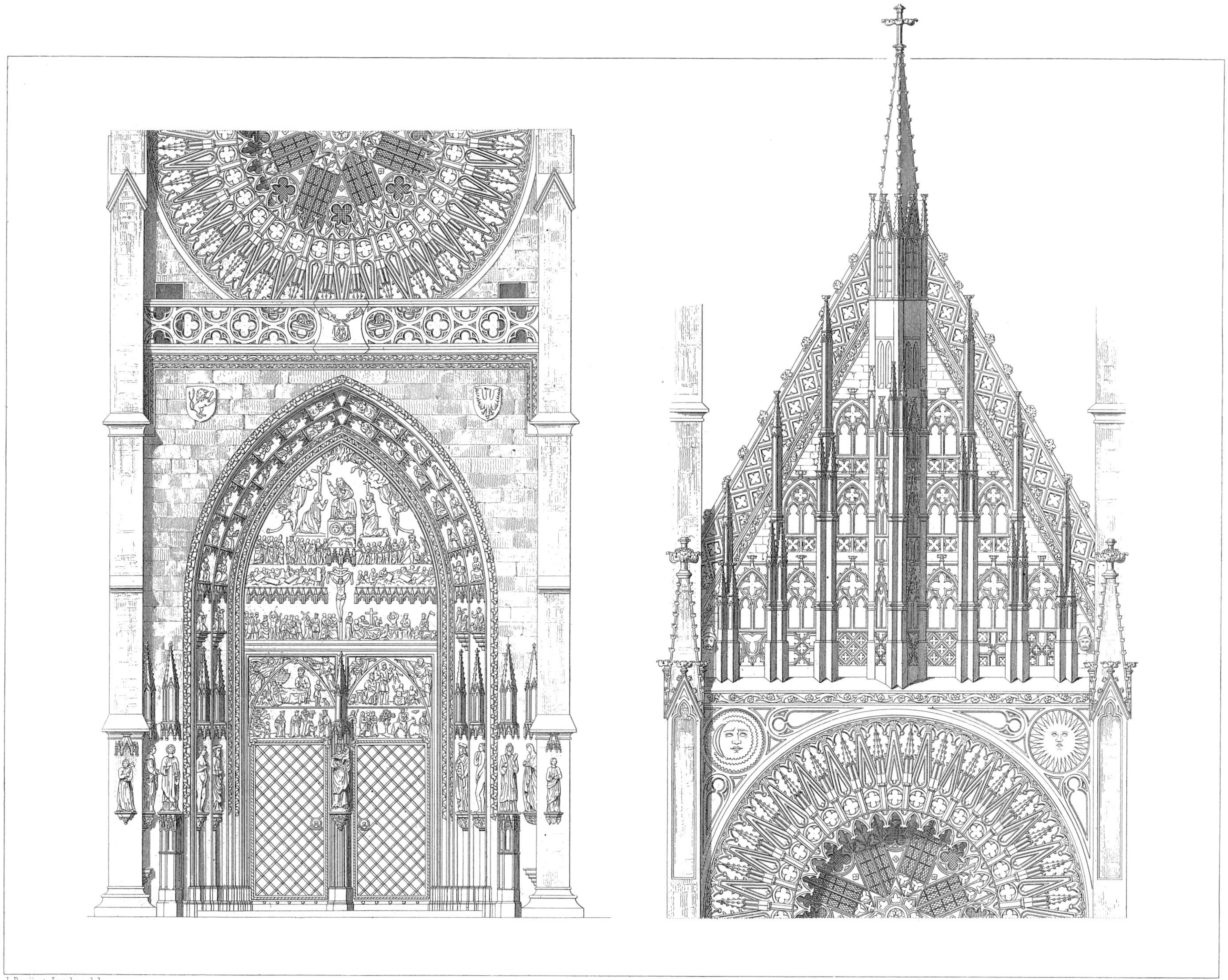

J. Burÿ et Jourdan del. J. Burÿ et Lecocq sc

Plate 58

Church of St. Lawrence, Nuremberg, Germany

J. Jourdan del.

Bury sculp.

Plate 59

Church of St. James of Scotland, Regensburg, Germany

Amondru del.

Bury sculp.

Plate 60

Cathedral, Speyer, Germany

Amoudru. del.

Bury sculp.ᵗ

Plate 61

Speyer Cathedral
Interior View

Plate 62

Speyer Cathedral
Plan and Cross Section

Amoudru d

Bury sculp.t

30 Metres

Plate 63

Speyer Cathedral
Longitudinal Section

Fig. 3.

Fig. 4.

Fig. 5.

Fig. 6.

Fig. 7.

Fig. 8.

Fig. 9.

Fig. 10.

Fig. 11.

Fig. 2.

Fig. 1.

Echelle des Détails.

1   2   3 Mètres.

Echelle pour la Crypte.

Amoudru del.

Bury sculp.t

Plate 64

Speyer Cathedral
Details

Plate 65

Cathedral, Trier, Germany

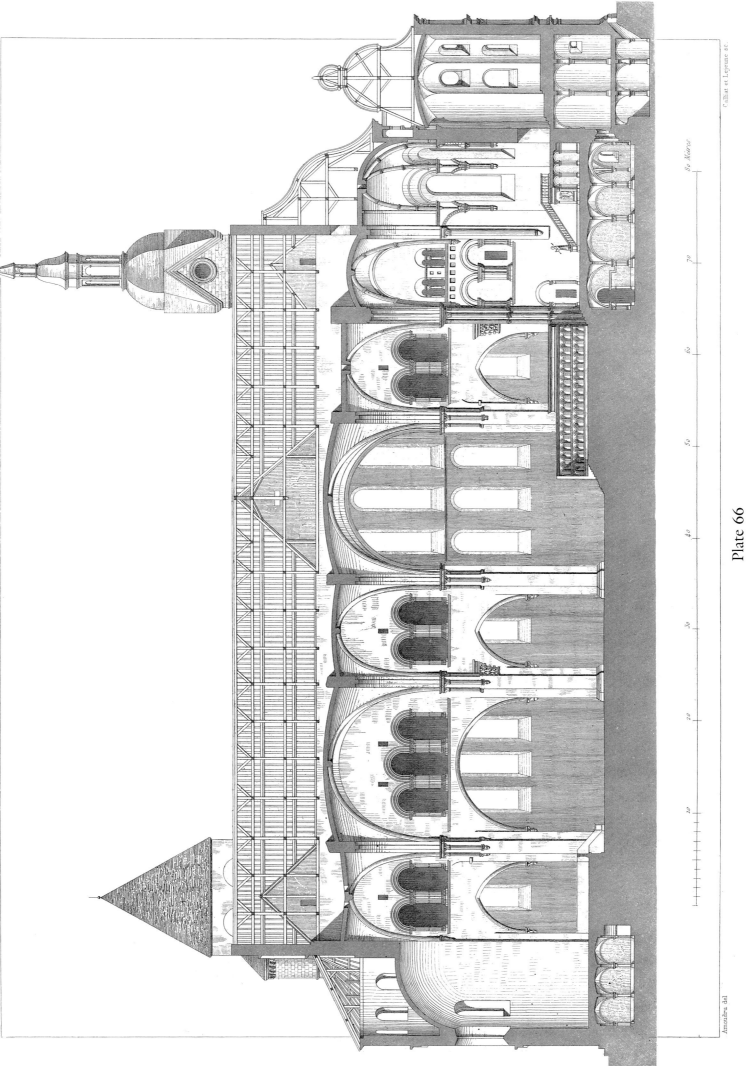

Plate 66

Trier Cathedral
Longitudinal Section

80 Mètres

Fig. 1.

Fig. 8.

Fig. 2.

Fig. 3.

Fig. 8.

Fig. 4.

Fig. 5.

Fig. 9.

Fig. 6.

Fig. 7.

1 Mètre.

Amoudru del.

Pfnor sculpt.

Plate 67

Trier Cathedral
Details

Fig. 4.

Fig. 3.

Fig. 1.

Fig. 2.

3 Metres

Plate 68

Trier Cathedral
Screen

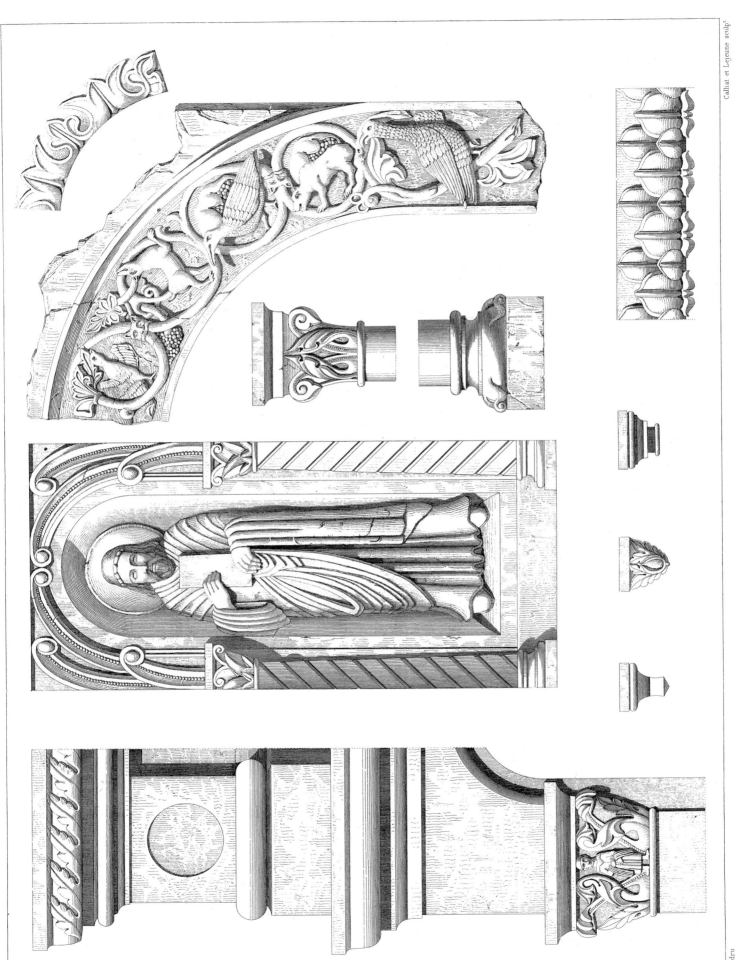

Plate 69

Trier Cathedral
Details, Enclosure of the Choir

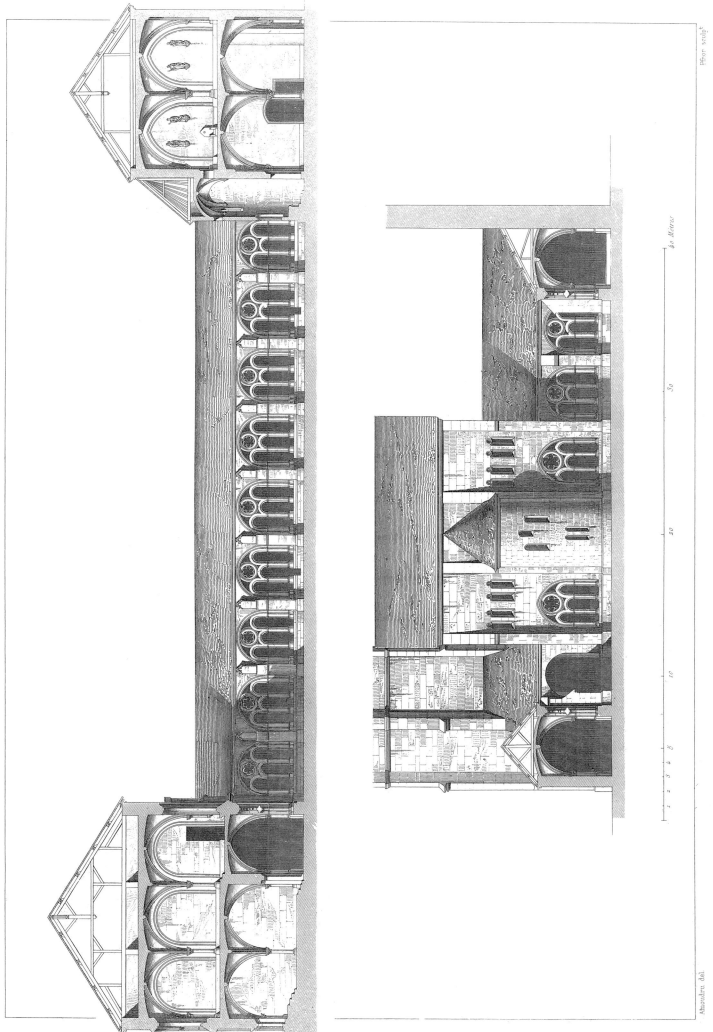

Plate 70

Trier Cathedral
Elevations (Cloister)

Ab. Lenoir del.

J.Bury sculp.

Plate 71

Cathedral, Athens, Greece

Fig. 8

Fig. 6

Fig. 6

Fig. 3

Fig. 9

Fig. 4

Fig. 5

Fig. 1

0   30   50 Mètres

Fig. 2

10   0   10   20   30   40   50 Mètres

Fig. 7

Alb. Lenoir del.

J. Bury sc.

Plate 72

Athens Cathedral
Details

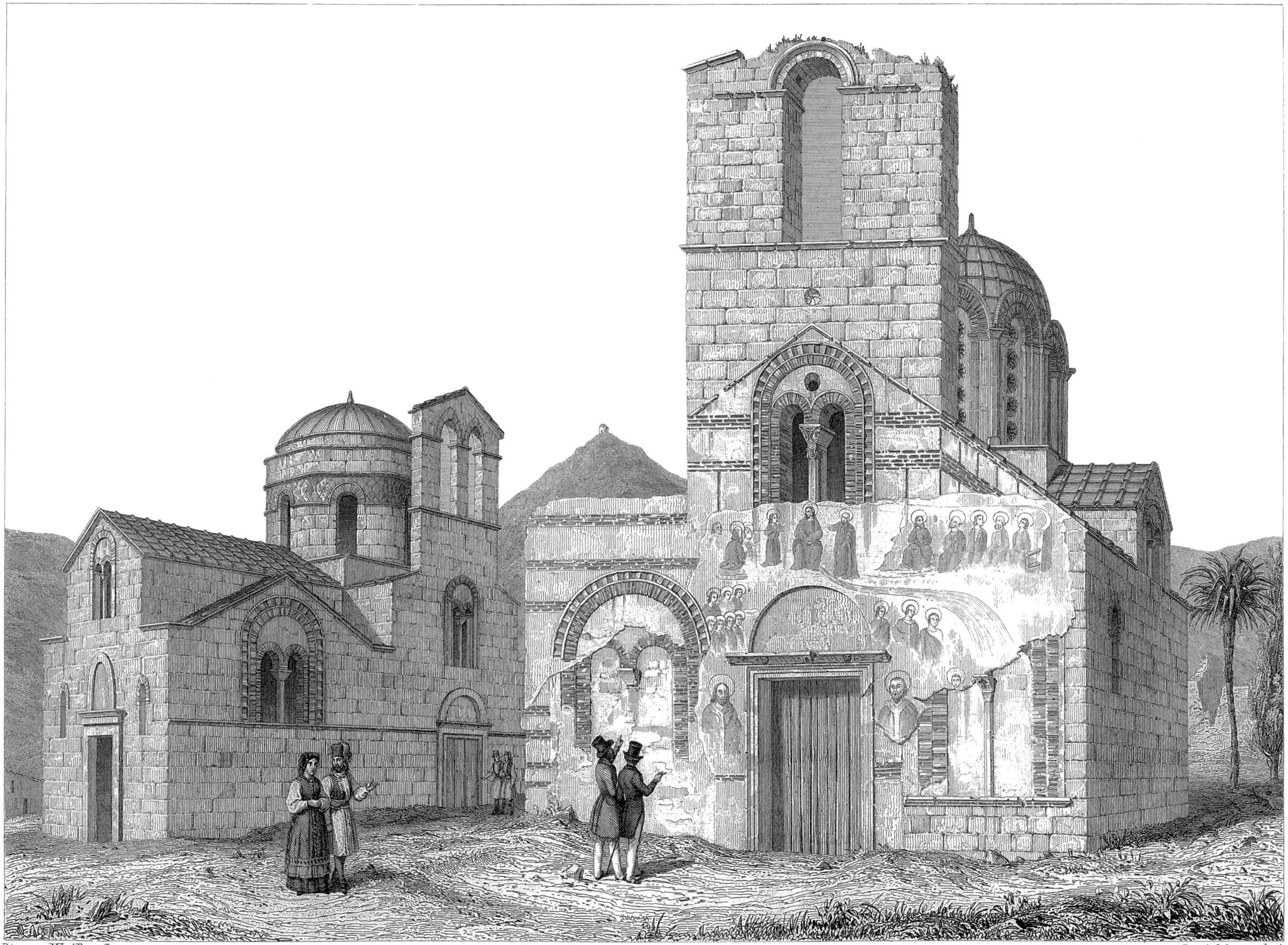

D'apres M^r. Albert Lenoir — Bury del. et sculps^t

Plate 73

Church of St. Taxiarque, Athens, Greece

Plate 74

Church of St. Francis, Assisi, Italy

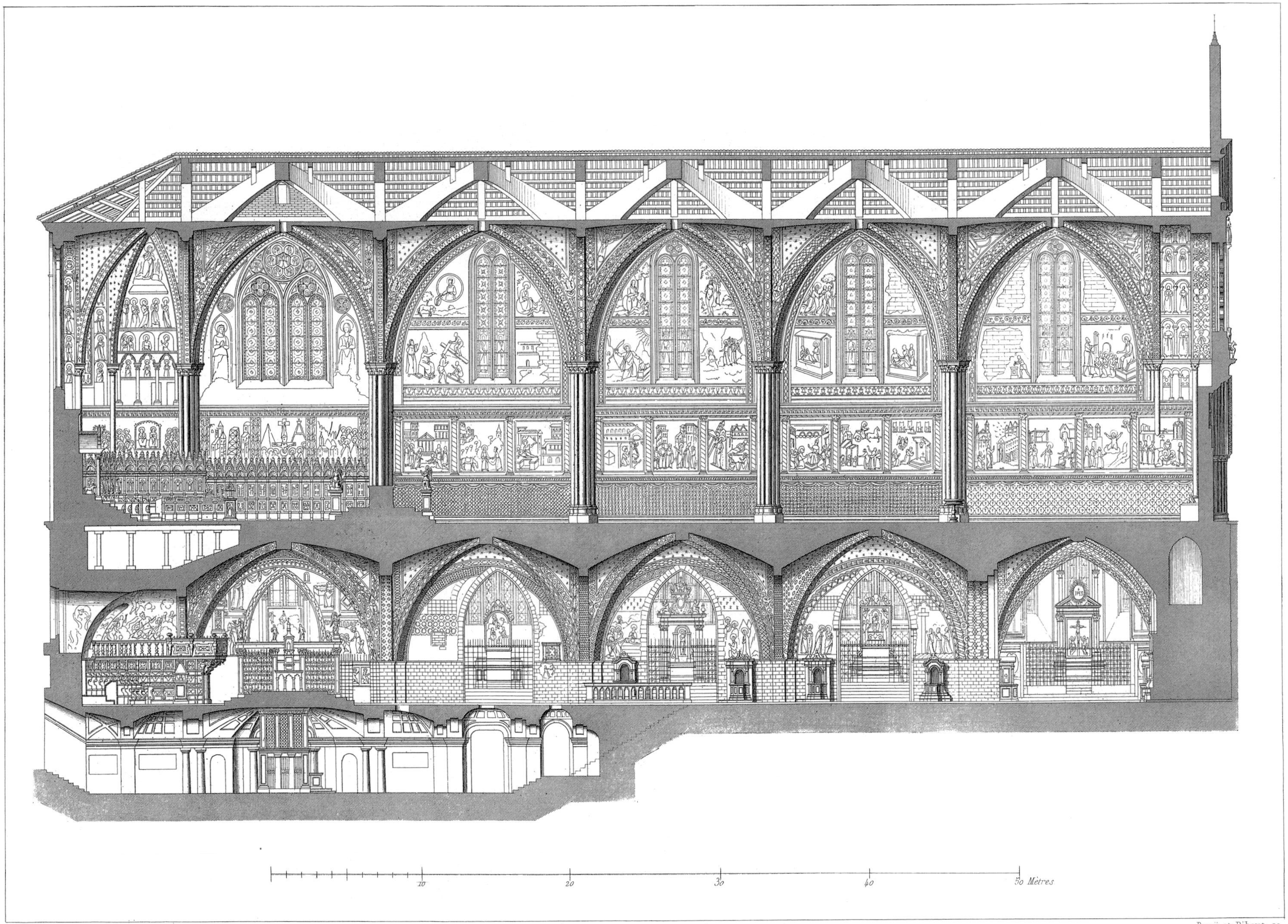

Plate 75

Church of St. Francis
Longitudinal Section

50 Metres

40

30

20

10

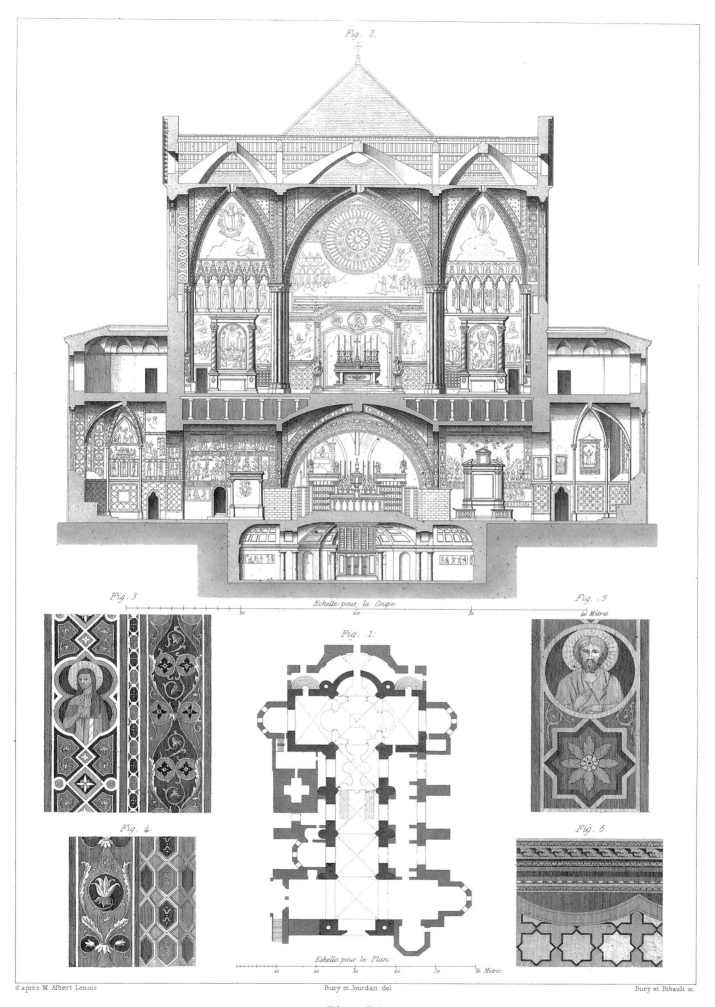

Fig. 2.

Fig. 3.   Echelle pour la Coupe   Fig. 5.

Fig. 1.

Fig. 4.   Fig. 6.

Echelle pour le Plan

Plate 76

Church of St. Francis
Details

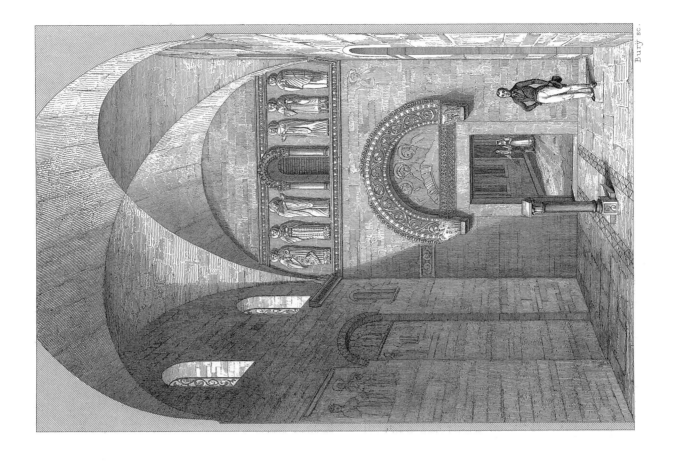

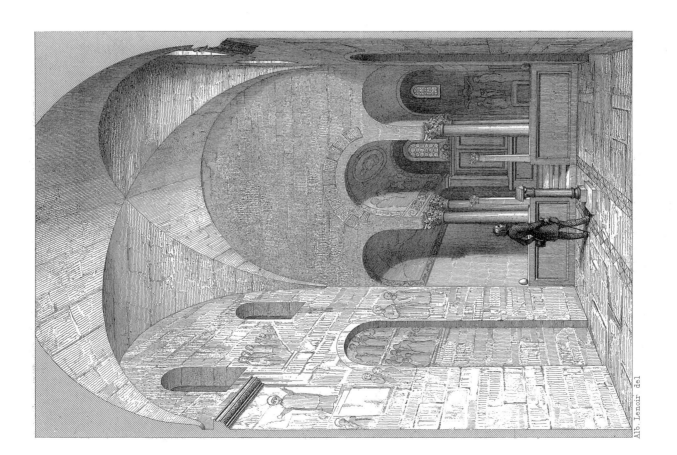

Plate 77

Chapel, Cividale del Friuli, Italy

Fig. 5.

Fig. 4.

Fig. 6.

Fig. 10.

Fig. 3.

Fig. 1.

Fig. 2.

Echelle pour le Plan

1   2   3   4   5 Mètres

Fig. 7.

Fig. 9.

Fig. 8.

Plate 78

Chapel, Cividale del Friuli
Details

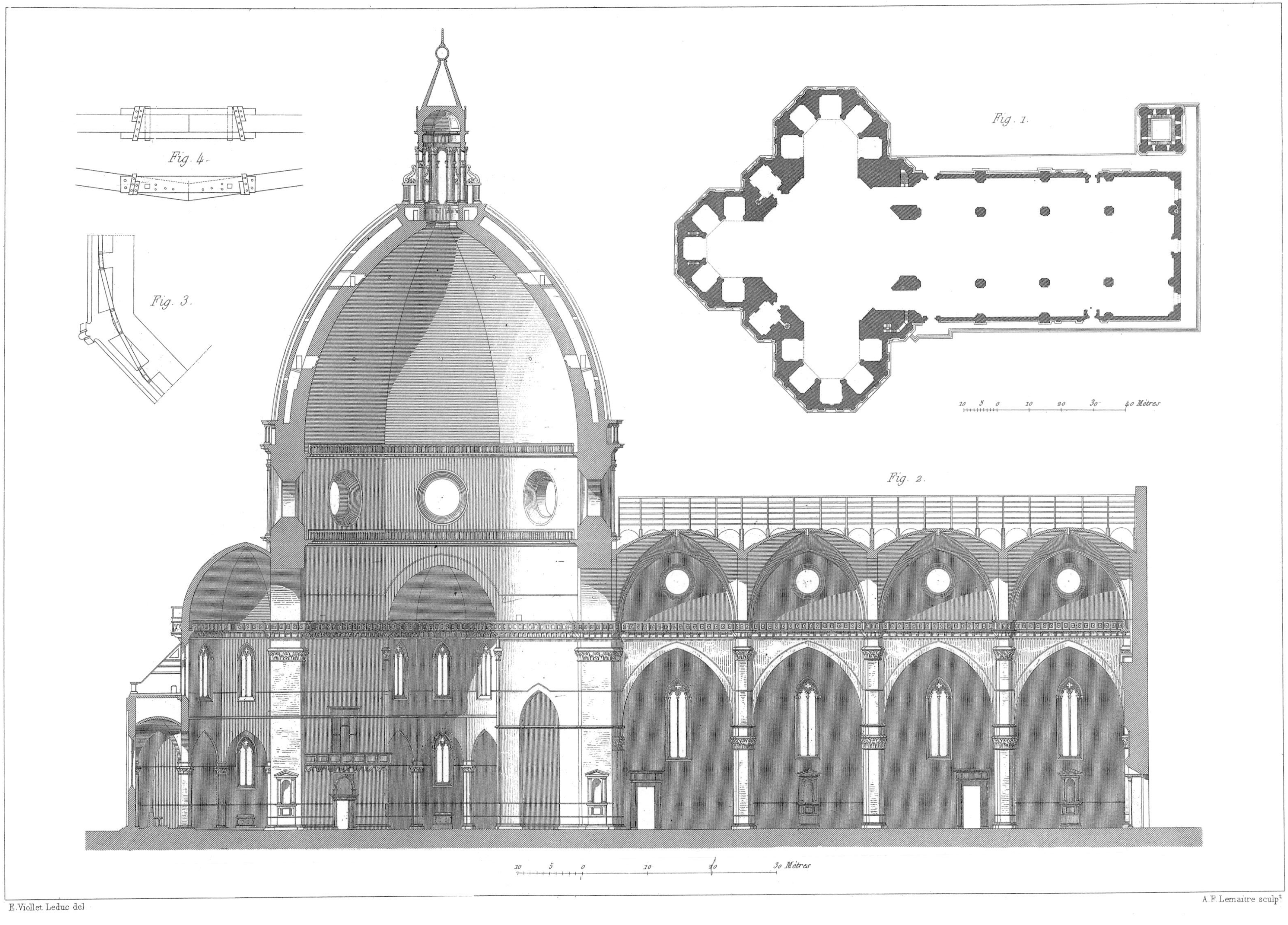

Fig. 1.
10 5 0 10 20 30 40 Mètres
Fig. 2.
10 5 0 10 20 30 Mètres
Fig. 3.
Fig. 4.
E. Viollet Leduc del
A. F. Lemaitre sculpt

Plate 79

Church of St. Mary-of-the-Flowers, Florence, Italy
Plan and Section

0   1   2   3   4   5   10 mètres

Plate 80

Church of St. Mary-of-the-Flowers
Lateral Elevation

E. Viollet Leduc del.

Lemaître et Schaal sc.

Fig. 1.

Fig. 2.

0   1   2   3   4   5   10 mètres

Plate 81

Church of St. Mary-of-the-Flowers
Lateral Elevation (Doors and Window)

Fig. 4.

Fig. 5.

Fig. 7.

Fig. 6.

Fig. 1.

Fig. 2.

Fig. 8.

Fig. 3.

Plate 82

Church of St. Mary-of-the-Flowers
Details, Campanile

Plate 83

Church of St. Miniato near Florence, Italy

Plate 84

Church of St. Miniato
Interior View

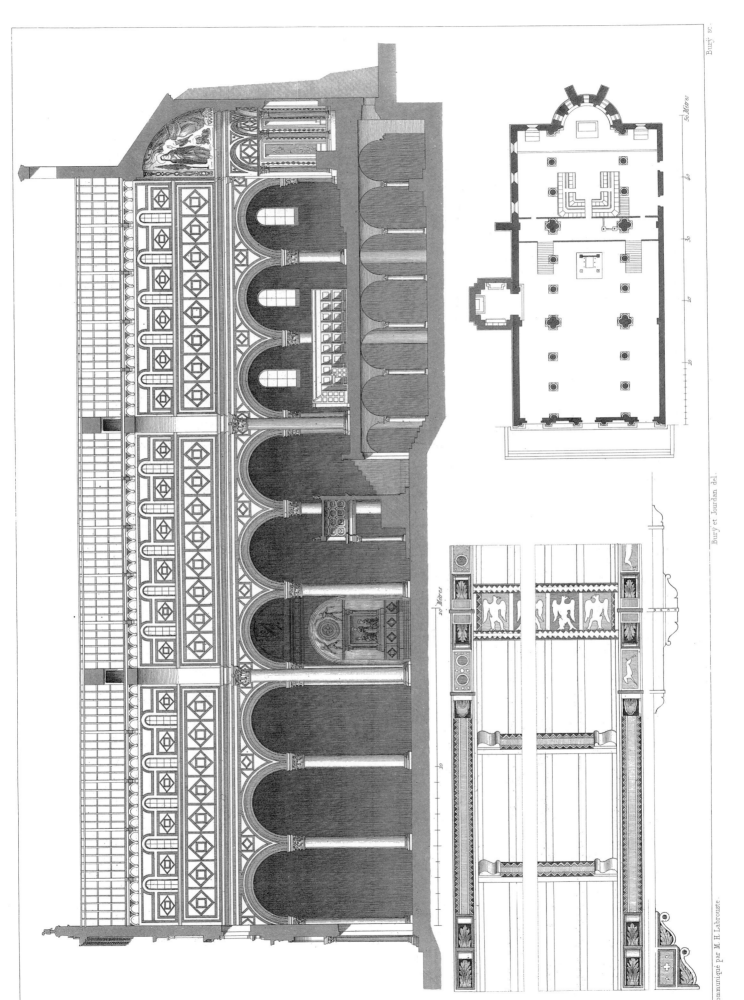

Bury et Jourdan del.

Bury sc.

Plate 85

Church of St. Miniato
Details

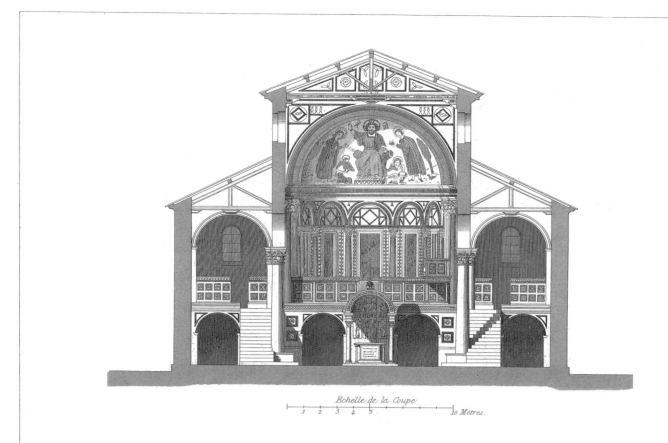

Communiqué par M. H. Labrouste.

Echelle de la Coupe

1 2 3 4 5   10 Mètres.

Fig. 2.

Fig. 4.

Fig. 3.

Fig. 5.

Fig. 1.

Bury et Jourdan del.

Bury. sc.

Plate 86

Church of St. Miniato
Details

Plate 87

Golden Church of San Michele, Florence, Italy
Tabernacle

d'après Edmond Prestat.

Plate 88

Golden Church of San Michele
Detail, Tabernacle

Plate 89

Church of Grotta-Ferrata, Italy

Jourdan & Burÿ del.

Plate 90

Cathedral, Palermo, Sicily, Italy
Elevation of Apse

d'après Mr Albert Lenoir   Jourdan del   J. Burÿ sc.

Plate 91

Church of La Martorana, Palermo, Sicily

Fig 5.

Fig. 4.

Fig. 3.

Fig. 1.

Fig. 7.

Fig. 6.

Fig. 8.

Fig. 9.

Fig. 2.

D'après M^r. Alb. Lenoir.

Jourdan del.

Bury sculp^t

Plate 92

Church of La Martorana
Details

E. Travers del.   Bury sculp!

Plate 93

Palatine Chapel, Palermo, Sicily

Fig. 4.

Fig. 5.

Fig. 2.

Fig. 1.

Fig. 8.

Fig. 3.

Fig. 7.

Fig. 9.

Fig. 10.

Fig. 6.

Echelle pour la Coupe

10 Mètres

Plate 94

Palatine Chapel
Details

Bury et Ribaut sc.t

W. Travers del.

Fig. 14.

Fig. 3.

Fig. 11.

Fig. 12.

Fig. 8.

Fig. 13.

10 Meters

Echelle pour les deux Coupes

Plate 95

Palatine Chapel
Details

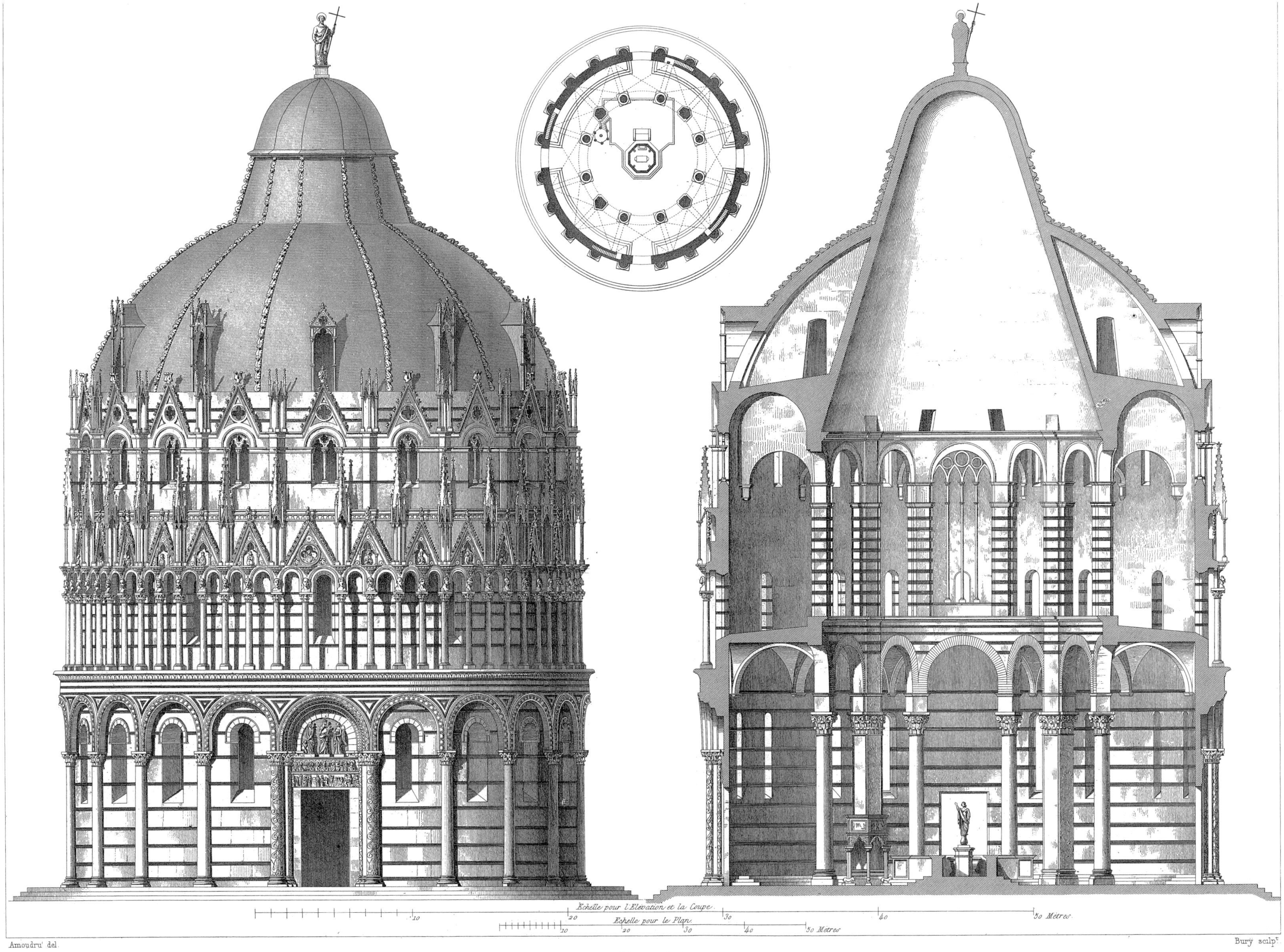
Échelle pour l'Élévation et la Coupe
10
20
30
40
50 Mètres
Échelle pour le Plan
10
20
30
40
50 Mètres
Amoudru del.
Bury sculp.t

Plate 96

Baptistery, Pisa, Italy

d'apres M. Isabelle   Larbalestier sculp.

Plate 97

Church of St. Vitale, Ravenna, Italy

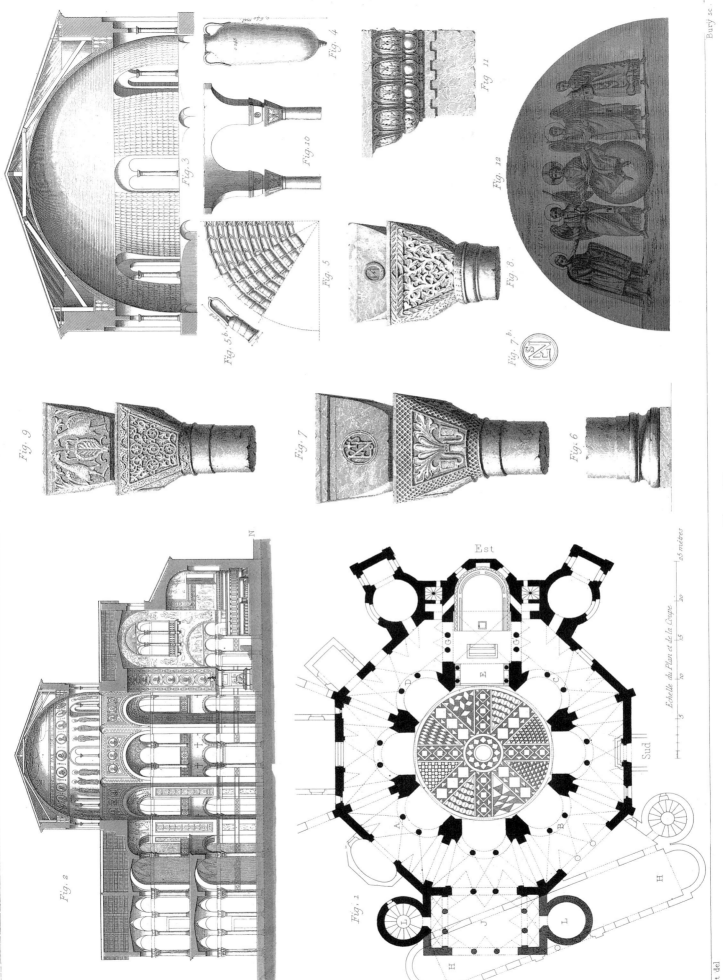

Fig. 2

Fig. 3

Fig. 4

Fig. 10

Fig. 11

Fig. 12

Fig. 9

Fig. 7

Fig. 6

Fig. 5

Fig. 5ᵇ·

Fig. 8

Fig. 7ᵇ·

Fig. 1

Est

Sud

Echelle du Plan et de la Coupe.

Bouchet del

Bury sc.

Plate 98

Church of St. Vitale
Details

Fig. 2.

Fig. 5.

Fig. 3.

Fig. 6.

Fig. 1.

Fig. 4.

Echelle pour la Figure 1.

10   20   30   40   50   60 *Metres.*

Echelle pour la Fig. 2.

1   2   3   4   5   6   7   8   9   10 *Met.*

Amoudru del.   d'après Mr Isabelle.   Bury sculp^t

Plate 99

Baptistery and Tomb of St. Constantia, Rome, Italy

Plate 100

Basilica of St. Clement, Rome, Italy

J. Bouchet del.

E. Ollivier sculp.

Plate 101

Basilica of St. Clement
Details

Echelle pour le Plan

50 Mètres

T·STEFANUS

J. Burý et Jourdan del.

J. Burý sculp.

Plate 102

Basilica of St. George of Vélabre, Rome, Italy

d'après Mr Alb. Lenoir .

Jourdan et Bury del

Bury et Schrœder sc

Plate 103

Basilica of St. George of Vélabre, Rome

Plate 104

Basilica of St. George of Vélabre
Ciborium

E. Viollet Leduc del.

Bury sculp.

Fig. 4. Fig. 3. Fig. 6. Fig. 7. Fig. 5. Fig. 8. Fig. 9. Fig. 10. Fig. 1. Fig. 2.

Plate 105

St. Lawrence's Church Outside the Walls of Rome
Episcopal Throne

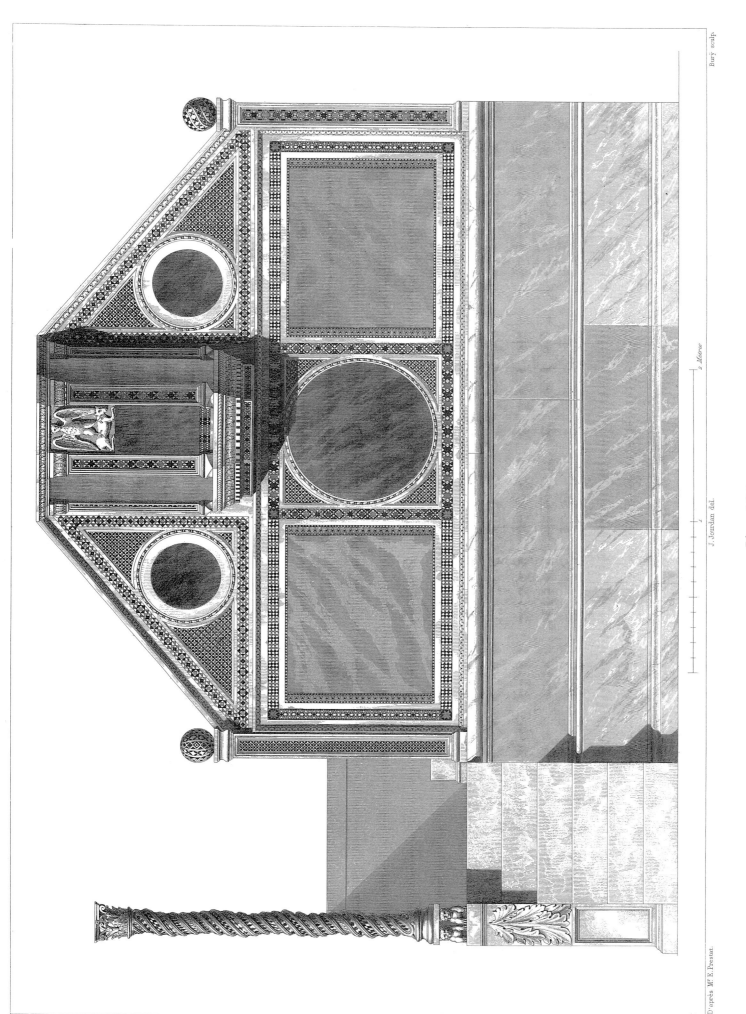

D'après M.E. Prestat.

J.Jourdan del.

Bury sculp.

2 Metre

Plate 106

St. Lawrence's Church Outside the Walls of Rome
Pulpit

Plate 107

Basilica of St. Marie in Cosmedin, Rome

Jourdan del

Bury sculps.

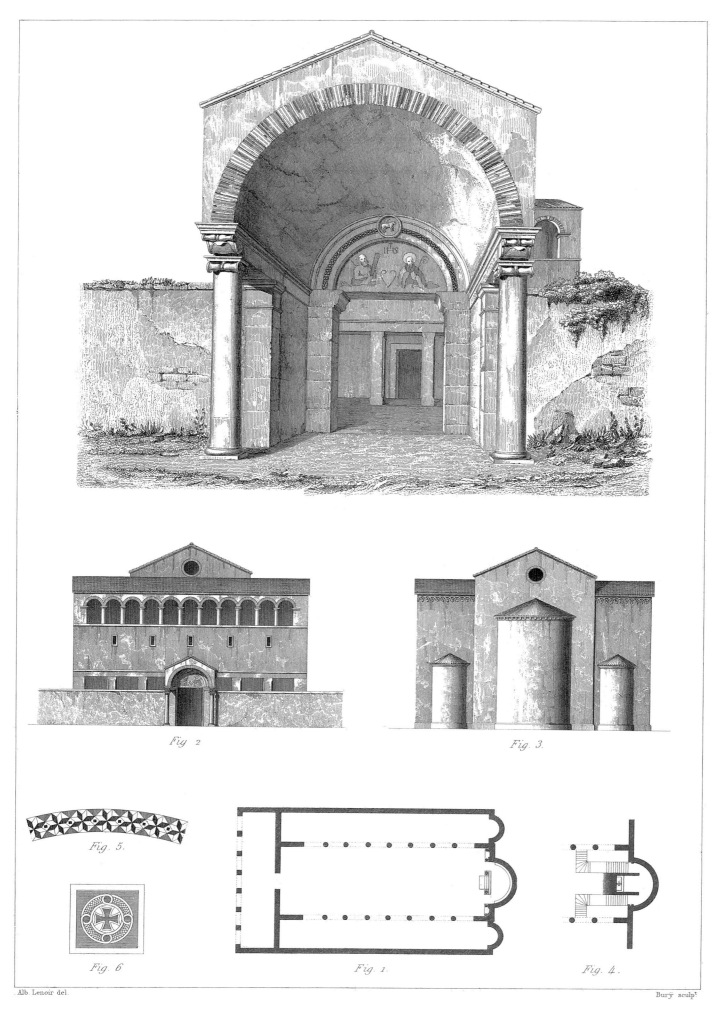

Fig 2

Fig. 3.

Fig. 5.

Fig. 6

Fig. 1.

Fig. 4.

Alb. Lenoir del.

Burÿ sculp.ᵗ

Plate 108

Basilica of St. Saba, Rome

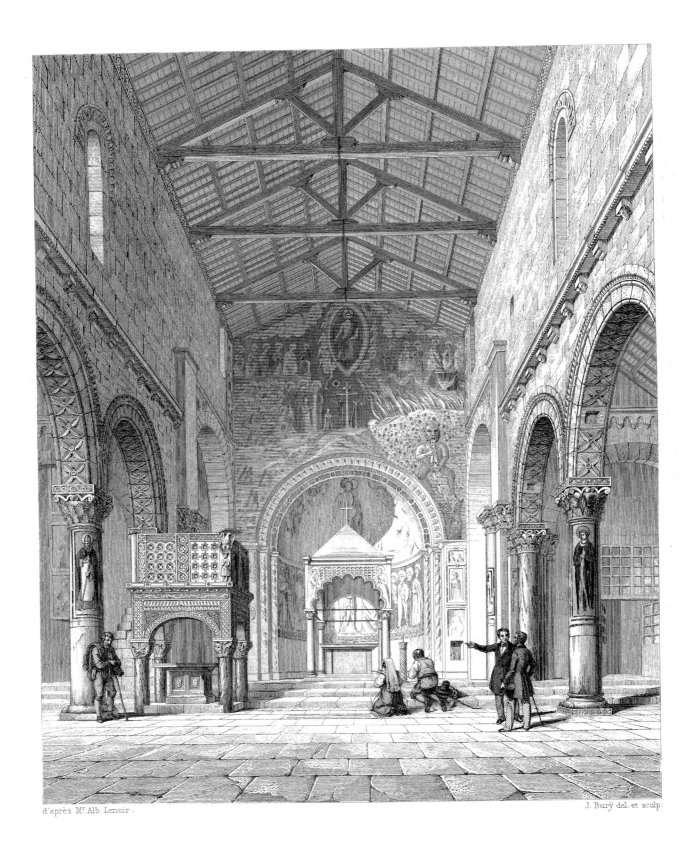

d'après Mr Alb. Lenoir.

J. Burÿ del. et sculp.

Plate 109

St. Mary's Church, Toscanella, Italy

Porte de gauche

Porte de droite

Echelle du Plan

5   10   15   20   25   30   35   40 mètres

d'après Mr Alb. Lenoir.

J. Bury del. et sc.

Plate 110

St. Mary's Church, Toscanella
Details

Plate 111

St. Mary's Church, Toscanella
Pulpit and Baptismal Fonts

J. Bury del. et sc.

d'après M. Alb. Lenoir

Plate 112

St. Mary's Church, Toscanella
Grand Portal

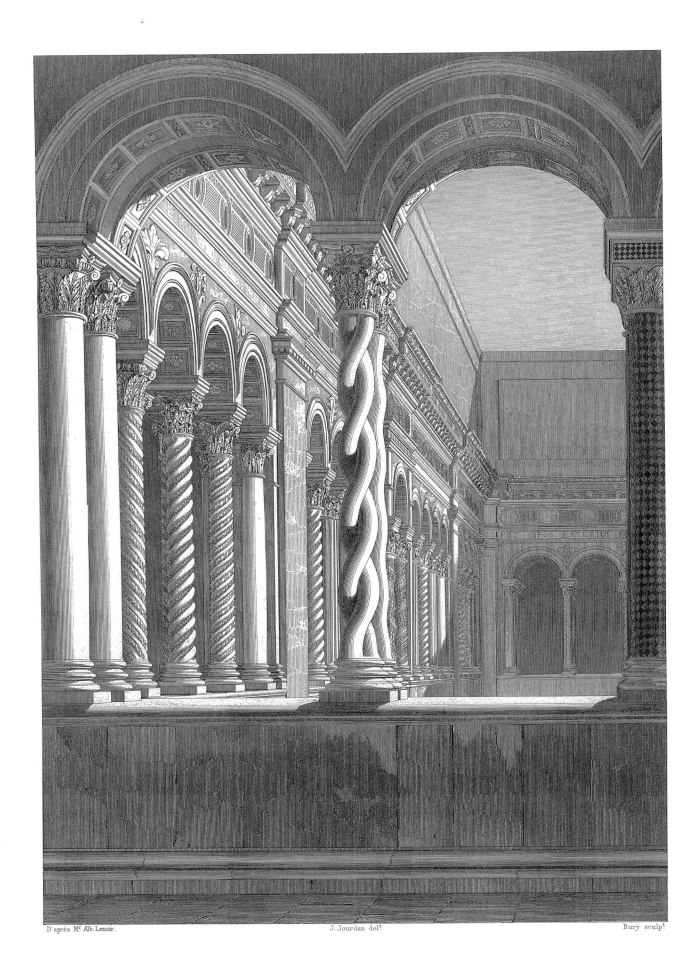

Plate 113

Church of St. Paul Outside the Walls of Rome
Cloister

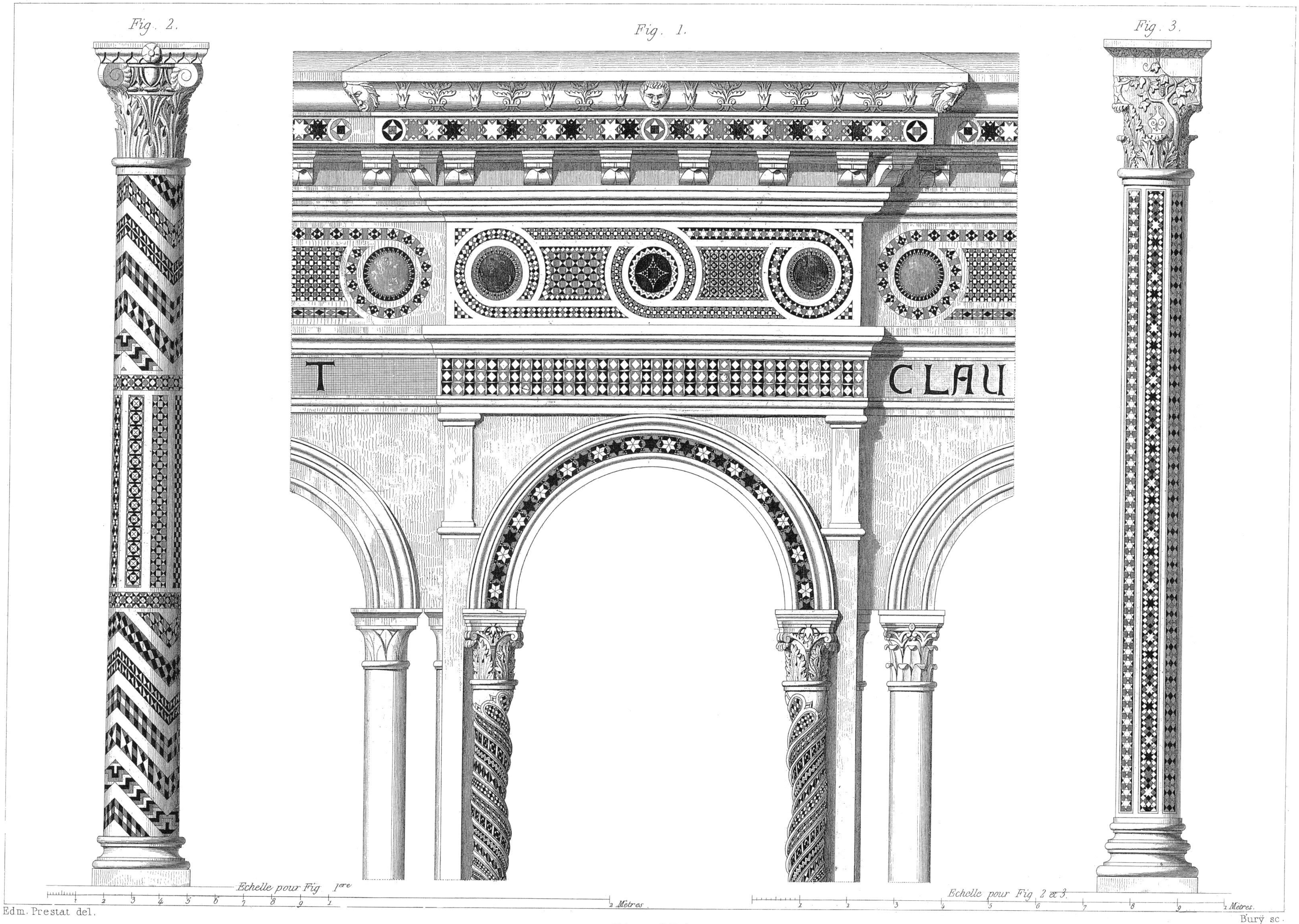
Fig. 1.
Fig. 2.
Fig. 3.
T
CLAU
Echelle pour Fig. 1ere
2 Mètres
Echelle pour Fig. 2 et 3.
2 Mètres
Edm. Prestat del.
Bury sc.

Plate 114

Church of St. Paul Outside the Walls of Rome
Details, Cloister

Fig. 1.

Fig. 2.

Plate 115

Church of St. Paul Outside the Walls of Rome
Details, Ciborium

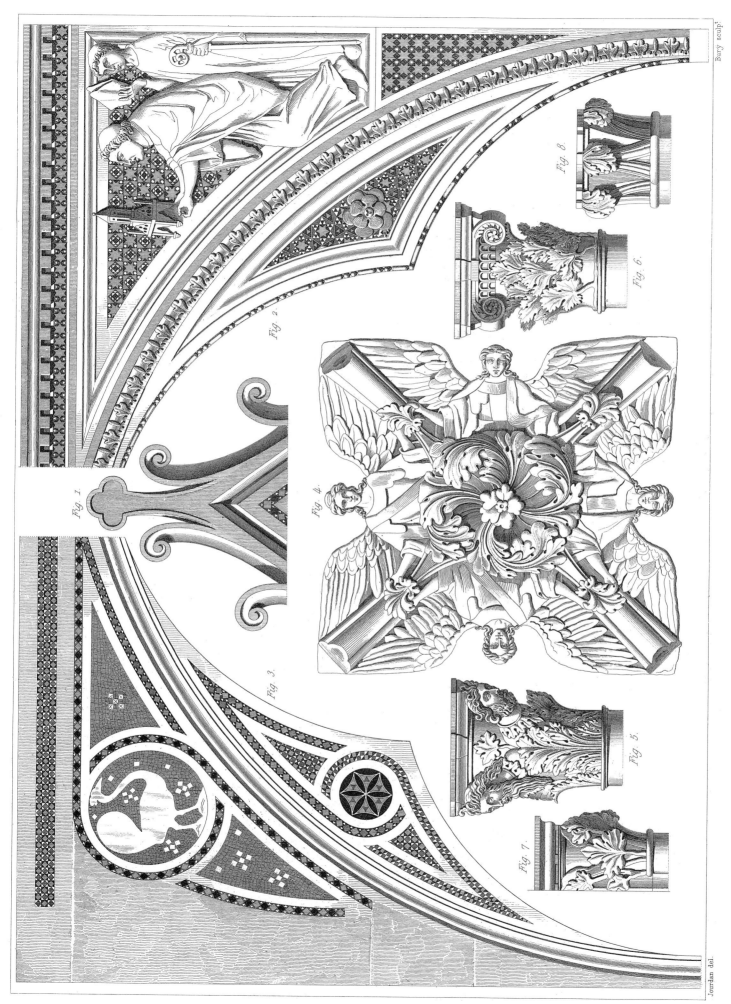

Fig. 1.

Fig. 2.

Fig. 3.

Fig. 4.

Fig. 5.

Fig. 6.

Fig. 7.

Fig. 8.

Plate 116

Church of St. Paul Outside the Walls of Rome
Details, Ciborium

d'après Quaglio

Burÿ et Thomas sc.

Plate 117

Cathedral of Bâle, Switzerland

Fig. 1

Fig. 2

Echelle pour l'élevation et la Coupe

2   1   2   3   4   5   20 Mètres

Fig. 3.   *Fig. 4.*   *Fig. 5.*

D'après Mr Albert Lenoir.   Bury et Jourdan del   Bury sculp¹

Plate 118

Church of Theotocos, Istanbul, Turkey
Facade and Narthex

Fig. 1.

Fig. 2.

Fig 4

Fig. 3.

Fig. 5.

Echelle pour l'Elevation et Coupe

10 Mètres

Echelle pour le Plan

20 Mètres

D'après M⁻ Alb. Lenoir.

Burÿ et Jourdan del.

Burÿ sculp

Plate 119

Church of Theotocos
Details

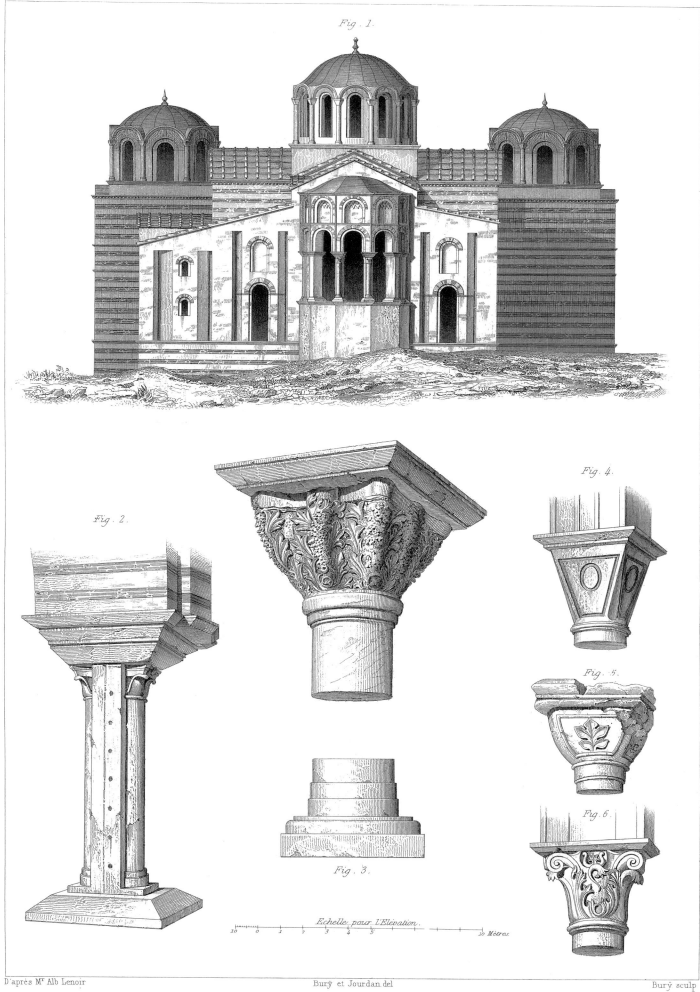

Fig. 1.

Fig. 2.

Fig. 4.

Fig. 5.

Fig. 6.

Fig. 3.

Echelle pour l'Elévation.

10   0   1   2   3   4   5   10 Mètres.

D'après Mr. Alb Lenoir   Burÿ et Jourdan del   Burÿ sculp

Plate 120

Church of Theotocos
Details

Index of Churches and Cathedrals